Quality Score in High Resolution™

Quality Score in High Resolution

Details, Secrets, and Insights on the Metric
that Can Make or Break Your PPC Results

Craig Danuloff

Potato Creek Books

Durham Pennsylvania

Quality Score in High Resolution
www.highresolutionppc.com
info@highresolutionppc.com

ISBN: 978-0615479385
First Paperback Printing - June 2011

Benefactors

This publication of this book was made possible in part by one-hundred wise, kind, good looking, and enthusiastic supporters including those listed below. Each has my gratitude and the thanks of everyone who has ever bid on a keyword.

David Szetela

Nikos Kapsomenakis

Hope Foster-Reyes

Jordan Glasner

Magne Uppman

Ulf Weihbold

Paul Robinson

Thomas Demers

Brandon Schmitz

James Zolman

Andy Ketter

Avinash Kaushik

Amy Moore

James Svoboda

Jordon Meyer

Raul Abad

Adrien O'leary

Enrique del valle

Magne Uppman

Frederik Trovatten

Dennis Ramm

Acknowledgements

I'd like to thank everyone at ClickEquations Inc. for all of their efforts and support of this project, including Lucinda Holt, Joanne Kondan, Alex Cohen and Adam Figueira who reviewed early drafts and provided important ideas and feedback.

Brad Geddes, David Szetela, Kim Clinkunbroomer, Richard Fergie, and Bryan Eisenberg provided valuable advice, reviews and comments.

Thanks to Dr. Siddharth Shah and Efficient Frontier Inc. for their kind permission to use some of the charts included in this book. Also to Rachael Haimowitz for her excellent copy editing and assistance.

Support from Google

Members of Google's Ads Quality Team were gracious enough to participate in interviews and answer written questions during the research and preparation of this book. In particular, I am indebted to Frederick Vallaeys who provided his time, support, and enthusiasm throughout this project.

Google's assistance was invaluable in helping me to understand and explain many of the formerly thorny parts of how quality score is calculated, how it's applied, and how best to manage quality score in your account. I sincerely appreciate their efforts in helping to make this book as complete and accurate as possible.

It should be noted, however, that while Google did review and comment on a near-final draft of the book, they did not in any way certify all of the content in this book. Any errors herein are my own.

Introduction

Google AdWords is an auction, but it doesn't work the way you might expect. In an AdWords auction, the highest bidder doesn't always win, and the amount you pay is based on a number of factors in addition to your bid.

These and other potentially unexpected results occur because the winners and fees in an AdWords auction are based upon a combination of bid *and* quality score, rather than just the bid itself. In fact, we would argue that the quality score a keyword earns is the single most influential factor on the ultimate success or failure of that keyword.

Google describes quality score as "an objective measurement of quality" that reflects how suitable and satisfying a keyword and its associated text ad are to people whose searches are matched to that keyword. The more likely Google thinks it is that an ad will get clicked, the higher the resulting quality score.

We know that the calculation of quality score is complex, but Google does not disclose the precise formula. Instead, they share only some basic information about how quality score is calculated and offer loose guidelines advertisers can use to try to obtain the best quality score possible.

Unfortunately, the official information is less than entirely clear, complete, or forthright. And the internet is filled with half-truths, assumptions, interpretations, silliness, rumors, and bad advice. As a result, many paid search managers have rather vague and simplistic notions about quality score, and very few know how to manage it well.

This book gathers the known truth, establishes some new truth, clarifies things that are probably true but haven't been officially confirmed, and debunks a lot of untruths.

Our goal is to provide the most complete and accurate collection of quality score information available anywhere. We also hope to provide clear and actionable recommendations about effectively creating and managing paid search accounts while maximizing quality scores and profit.

Successful paid search depends on successful quality score management. This book is your key to that success.

Contents

Part I: Introducing Quality Score

Chapter One:
The Quality Score Quick Tour   19

What Is Quality Score? **19**
    Driving Advertisers Toward Best Practices 20
    Everybody Wins.. 20
How Is Quality Score Calculated? **21**
    The Evolving Nature of the Quality Score Calculation 22
Where Is Quality Score Used? **23**
How Can You Improve Quality Scores? **24**
    Setup for Good Quality Scores 24
    Earn High Click-through Rates 26
    Avoid Penalties that Sabotage Quality Scores................................... 28
    The Simple Prescription for Good Quality Scores 30
Chapter Summary..**32**
    Disclaimer 33

Chapter Two:
The Official Words on Quality Score   35

Google Defines Quality Score **36**
    What It Means... 37
Google Justifies Quality Score **37**
    What It Means... 37
Google on the Factors that Influence Quality Score **39**
    What It Means... 39
Google on How Quality Score Impacts Your Account **40**
    What It Means... 40
What Google Doesn't Say about Quality Score **41**
    Filling in the Blanks, with Google's Help 42
Subject to Change **42**
Chapter Summary..**43**

Chapter Three:
The Role of Quality Score in AdWords   45

Quality Score as Preferred Customer Program...46
Quality Score as a Bozo Filter...46
   Accidental Bozos.. 46
   Intentional Bozos 47
   Paying the Bozo Tax.. 48
Quality Score as Secret Sauce 49
   Addressing Concerns without Answering Questions................................... 52
Chapter Summary...54

Chapter Four:
Which Quality Score?   55

The Quality Scores...56
The Details of Visible Quality Score...57
   How Visible Quality Score Is Unique.. 58
The Component Quality Scores 61
Quality Score on Google and Beyond...62
Chapter Summary...63

Part II:
Understanding Quality Score

Chapter Five:
How Quality Score Is Calculated   67

The Factors that Influence Quality Score..68
Factor #1: Click-through Rate 69
   Meet the Click-through Rates 69
   Historical CTR of the Keyword and Matched Ad.................................... 70
    What about New or Modified Text Ads?...72
   Historical CTR of the Account.. 72
    The Myth of Ad-Group Quality Score...74
   Historical CTR of
   Display URLs... 74
   Geographical Performance 76
   Other CTR Factors 77
   The Role of Visible CTR in Quality Score 79
    How Keyword CTR Correlates with Visible Quality Score...........................80

Factor 2: Relevance **82**
   The Secret of Relevance...*83*
   Why Google Says "Relevance" When They Mean CTR................*84*
   Reviewing Relevance Ratings *85*
  Two Kinds of Relevance 86
   Vertical Relevance...*86*
   Horizontal Relevance *87*
   Search Results without Paid Ads *88*
  Final Thoughts on Relevance.. 89
Factor 3: Landing Page Quality.....................................**90**
  Reviewing Landing Page and Site Quality 94
  The Impact of Landing Pages on Quality Score.................... 96
  How Often Are Landing Pages Reviewed?.......................... 97
  Last Thoughts On Landing Page Quality 98
Weighting the Quality Score Factors................................**99**

Chapter Summary..**100**
  Now See the Movie...102

Chapter Six:
The Impact of Quality Score   **103**

Quality Score Impact One:
Eligibility **105**
  Bid Requirements and Missed Auctions 106
   Tracking Missed Eligibility with Impression Share.................*107*

Quality Score Impact Two:
Ad Position..**108**
  Jumping to a Top Position...109

Quality Score Impact Three:
The Price You Pay...**110**
  How Much Does Quality Score Save or Cost 114
  When Ads Stand Alone 116

Quality Score Impact Four:
The First Page Bid Estimate...**116**

Chapter Summary..**119**

Chapter Seven:
The Numbers and What They Mean   **121**

Viewing Quality Score **122**

What Quality Score Numbers Mean **124**

Quality Scores 10, 9, and 8: The Great Ones.........................125
The Benefits of Excellent Quality Scores...............................*126*
Quality Score 7: The Standard 129
Quality Scores 6 and 5: Nearly Good Enough? 129
Quality Scores 4, 3, 2, and 1: The Stinkers............................130

How Are Quality Scores Distributed? **131**

Viewing Account-wide Quality Score Distributions **132**

Plotting Quality Score Distribution for Your Account..............134

How Often Are Quality Scores Updated? **135**

Chapter Summary..**136**

Part III:
Improving Quality Score

Chapter Eight:
The Simple Path to Good Quality Scores   **139**

The Quality Way **140**

The Quality Score Shortcut **142**

Step 1: Choose Appropriate Keywords 142
Associating Keywords with Intent...*143*
Keyword Caveats...*145*
Step 2: Organize Keywords into Tightly Focused Ad Groups 146
How Small Is Small Enough?...*149*
Step 3: Write Direct and Compelling Ad Copy 150
Keywords in Ad Copy..*151*
Dynamic Keyword Insertion..*152*
Conclusion...*153*
Step 4: Deliver a Great Landing Page Experience 153

Will the Quality Score Shortcut Work?....................................**155**

Chapter Nine:
Preparing to Manage Quality Score   157

Introducing Quality Score Management 157

An Account-wide View: Quality Score Bucket Analysis 159

Goals for Quality Score 162

   About Generalizations and Categorizations...163

Why Quality Scores Are Low 164

   Resolving Structural Problems *165*

   Resolving Keyword Issues or Overexpansion...*165*

   Working in Competitive Markets *166*

   Head Scratchers *167*

Keyword Perspectives 167

   Keyword Options 171

Quality Score Management Principles 172

Chapter Summary... 174

Chapter Ten:
Dealing with Disaster   175

Overcoming Business Model Penalties.. 176

   Repent and Recover..*178*

Resolving Landing Page Penalties... 179

Getting Clean / Verifying compliance 180

   Requesting Forgiveness: Contacting Google 182

Your AdWords Account Sucks 182

Starting Over with a New AdWords Account... 183

   When Rehab Is Better than Restart...185

   How to Restart...186

     Avoid Duplicate Accounts Trouble...*187*

     Start with Winners..*189*

     Expand Slowly...*190*

     Losers Not Allowed..*191*

   Moving Quality Scores..192

Chapter Summary... 193

Chapter Eleven:
Everyday Quality Score Management   195

What to Expect 195

Prioritizing Your Work 198

The Top Ten Ways to
Improve the Quality Score of Any Keyword 199
    Step 1: Rule out Landing Page Penalties 199
    Step 2: Rule out Poor Relevance 199
    Step 3: Rule out Slow Page Load Times 200
    Step 4: Decide if the Keyword Is Worth Fixing 200
    Step 5: Review and React to the Search Queries 201
    Step 6: Create Smaller Ad Groups 201
    Step 7: Write Better Ad Copy 202
    Step 8: Try a Higher Average Position 202
    Step 9: Consider a Different Display URL 203
    Step 10: Stop Running Ads in Poorly Performing Geographies 203
    Last Thoughts on the Ten-step Plan 204

Keyword Expansion and Query Mining 204
    Search Query Reports 205
    Last Thoughts on Query Mining 208

Fracturing Keywords for Quality Score Clues 209

When Keywords Are Too Targeted 210

Wave a White Flag 213

Chapter Summary 214

AfterWords   215

Imperfections 216

Managing Quality 217

Part I:
Introducing Quality Score

Chapter One:
The Quality Score Quick Tour

This book takes an exhaustive look at quality score. It's a complex subject with many implications for the practice of paid search management.

But before we delve too deep, let's cover the basic facts of quality score by answering four simple questions:

- What is quality score?
- How is quality score calculated?
- Where is quality score used?
- What can be done to improve and manage quality score?

What Is Quality Score?

Quality score is a rating AdWords assigns to each keyword in your account that reflects Google's assessment of how well that keyword is expected to perform. It is used to assist and encourage keywords that are expected to perform well, and to hinder and discourage keywords that are expected to perform poorly.

The "performance" that Google is focusing on is the likelihood that a given text ad associated with a specific keyword will satisfy searchers and earn their clicks. Perhaps not coincidentally, keywords that perform well based on this definition also maximize Google's earnings by generating more paid clicks from more happy users, who then search on Google more frequently.

Quality score is a prediction about the future based on the past. It's determined by a complex mathematical calculation whose variables include a wide range of information about the structure and performance of your account as a whole, and of your keywords, text ads, and landing pages in specific. There is no human subjectivity involved. Like any prediction, it's really just a best guess, but since it's a computer-generated guess, it's constantly recalculated as more history and better data become available.

DRIVING ADVERTISERS TOWARD BEST PRACTICES

Quality score also serves to encourage good advertising practices and discourage or prevent bad ones. The majority of the steps required to earn good quality scores are efforts that improve your advertising and help you to earn more money—things you'd want to do even if quality score wasn't being measured. But by measuring and reporting on these efforts via quality score, which itself impacts your results, Google is able to reward what they consider good behavior and punish what they consider bad behavior.

Quality score also helps Google to avoid or eliminate a lot of problems that would occur if they only considered bids when deciding the winner of an auction. If money were the only factor, many advertisers would bid based on demographics and context: seeking to get their ads shown to certain people or near certain topics. Automotive and beer ads would be shown for all sports-related keywords, pharmaceutical ads for all keywords related to the elderly, concert ticket and movie ads next to keywords young people might search, and so on.

There would also undoubtedly be a lot of ad copy that essentially tricked people into clicking. More than a few ads would promise or suggest something far different than would actually be delivered on the landing page that appears after the click. Some may even suggest easy access to sex, money, beer, or pizza, when in fact the landing page offers nothing more than a good deal on mortgage refinancing.

Quality score makes all of these tactics difficult and ultimately impossible.

EVERYBODY WINS

It's easy to be cynical about Google's motives with quality score by viewing it as a way to control and confuse advertisers and raise paid search prices. But the fact is that quality score is so important and successful because it actually benefits each of the participants in the AdWords ecosystem.

It's a win-win-win proposition.

♦ **Searchers Win:** Quality score helps AdWords deliver a good experience. If Google can predict which ads will satisfy users and show those ads more frequently, searchers are more likely to find what they want, have a good experience, return to Google frequently, and run lots of searches over time.

♦ **Advertisers Win:** Quality score helps AdWords deliver marketing success. If Google can show your ads more frequently in situations where they satisfy searchers, you'll gain traffic, buyers, and profits.

♦ **Google Wins:** Quality score helps AdWords make more money. If Google can show searchers satisfying ads that drive more searches, while at the same time help advertisers reach targeted prospects affordably enough to keep spending on AdWords, then Google makes more money.

Quality score helps you and your potential customers to be more efficient and effective, while at the same time helping Google to improve their business. It does present challenges and complexity, but these are offset by the benefits to both Google and advertisers.

How Is Quality Score Calculated?

Quality score is an attempt to predict the behavior and performance of your keyword, text ad, and landing page. It's designed to determine the degree to which these elements, as configured for a particular search query, are likely to:

♦ Satisfy the searcher (provide what they were looking for)

♦ Satisfy the advertiser (get lots of clicks)

♦ Satisfy Google (earn them a lot of money)

The following factors are the primary influences on quality score:

◆ **Click-through Rate**: Click-through rate (CTR) history is the most important component of quality score. This includes the CTR of specific keyword + ad copy combinations, the entire account, and the display URL in the text ad associated with the keyword.

◆ **Relevance**: Relevance is the second most important factor impacting quality score. Google is never particularly clear about what they mean by relevance, but most people assume it to be some kind of topical symmetry: a consistency of meaning or even an exactness of terminology between keywords, text-ad copy, landing pages, and the search queries they're matching. (The truth, it turns out, is a little different, as we'll explain and explore in *Chapter Five: How Quality Score Is Calculated*.)

◆ **Other Factors**: Quality score can also be influenced by a collection of other account and campaign attributes and named and un-named metrics. Google has only disclosed a few of these, such as the geographic location of the searcher, certain characteristics of the landing page used by the ad, and (in some cases) the advertiser's business model or market segment.

THE EVOLVING NATURE OF THE QUALITY SCORE CALCULATION

When an account is first created and new keywords and text ads are added, there isn't much data from which Google can determine appropriate quality scores. At the other end of the spectrum are accounts that have been open for years and are filled with keywords and text ads that have huge amounts of detailed history that can be considered. It's not surprising that Google treats these two differently. To make the matter even more complicated, new keywords or ad copy are often added into old accounts, so there are elements without any track record mixed in with with those that are well established.

To operate in this fluid environment, the quality score calculation is adaptable. When extensive CTR history for a specific keyword and ad copy combination is available, that data is weighted heavily. But if this data is not available, then other factors (such as historical account-wide CTR) are given more weight.

The process of calculating a quality score begins as soon as a new keyword is added to your account. AdWords immediately starts working to assign and define a quality score for it. If that keyword has no history in your account, then Google looks elsewhere for clues—such as the CTR history of the entire account, the CTR history of the visible URL, or even the historical CTR that keyword has produced for other advertisers. Over time, as the keyword gains impressions and a click-through rate emerges for it in combination with specific text ads, this direct evidence supplants the influence of other factors. Ultimately, as history is built up in specific geographies and with specific search queries, this history is taken into consideration and the weight of non-keyword specific measures decreases even further.

The popular notion of a single rigid formula for quality score just isn't true; instead, Google varies the calculation to make an accurate prediction based on the best information available to them at the time.

Where Is Quality Score Used?

Quality score has a huge impact on the results achieved in paid search accounts because quality score affects four important decisions that occur every time someone executes a search that may be related to any of your keywords:

1. **Whether or not your ad will be shown**. If the quality score of a particular keyword is too low, it can be disqualified as ineligible before an auction even begins.

2. **The "first page bid estimate" for that keyword**. The lower the quality score of any particular keyword, the higher the minimum bid estimate you'll be given to suggest how much you'll need to bid to win placement on the first page of the search results .

3. **The position in which your ad will appear in the search results**. Each keyword competes against those of other advertisers for space on the search results page, and quality score is one half of the formula used to determine the position in which the ads assigned

to those keywords will appear. A higher quality score has just as much weight as a higher bid in helping your ads rank above the competition.

4. **How much you'll be charged when your ads are clicked**. The quality score of your keywords works directly to raise or lower your cost per click (CPC). High quality scores save you money on every click, while low quality scores cost you money every time someone clicks on one of your ads.

In other words, quality score is pretty important! If you don't earn good or great quality scores, then your ads will appear less frequently and in lower positions on the page, and you will pay more for every resulting click.

How Can You Improve Quality Scores?

Since quality score is a quantified prediction for the success of a keyword, the best way to raise it is to do things that are likely to make the keyword successful. You can have a big impact by doing things that attract a high or increased volume of clicks.

The best way to get a lot of clicks is to: 1) setup for success, 2) earn high click-through rates, and 3) avoid penalties. In the sections below, we discuss the specific steps you can take to apply each of these ideas in your account.

1) Setup for Good Quality Scores

Good quality scores come from great click-through rates, and great click-through rates come from a tight alignment between what users are searching for and the ads they see. By ensuring that keywords, search queries, and ad copy are all contextually aligned—tightly focused on the same uber-narrow topic and using literally or essentially the same words to represent their idea—you make it more likely that the people who see your ads will click on them.

To maximize the alignment of queries, keywords, ad copy, and landing pages, you should avoid certain elements or configurations within your account. In particular:

♦ **Avoid generic keywords.** When a keyword has a broad meaning, such as a category name or a generic term, it tends to be matched to a huge range of different search queries. There are over 100,000 search queries that could reasonably be matched to the broad match keyword "notebook computer," for example. This huge funnel of search intent makes it very difficult to write ad copy that most of those searchers will find relevant, and therefore it's hard to get good CTRs for this type of keyword.

Unless you're advertising a brand that is dominant in a particular category, it's best to build your account with highly specific keywords that include two, three, four, or even more words. For instance, it's easy to create clearly aligned ad copy and landing pages for a keyword like "replacement battery for Dell Latitude notebooks". Build your account around this type of highly specific keyword, and only after your quality scores are strong and well established should you consider expanding toward more generic ones.

♦ **Avoid large ad groups.** Although it's possible to group up to 2,000 keywords together in a single ad group, you don't want to get anywhere near this limit unless you've come up with that many synonyms for the same root term. There's only one set of text ads in an ad group, and they're shown to every person who enters any search query that is matched to any keyword in that ad group. So the greater the number and diversity of keywords, the greater the range of search queries, and this huge diverse funnel all points to just a few ads. There is no way to keep ad copy as relevant to search queries in large ad groups as it is to queries in small ones.

♦ **Avoid generic text-ad copy**. After going to the trouble of organizing keywords into small, tightly-focused ad groups, it's then necessary to compose ad copy that's directly tailored to those keywords and the search queries they'll attract. When ad copy isn't specific, lower relevance leads to lower click-through rates.

♦ **Avoid generic landing pages, or at least generic visible URLs.** The visible display URL used in each text ad helps the user know what they're going to get after they click. By signaling with the visible URL and then sending users to highly relevant pages (don't send everyone to your home page—link as deeply into your site as possible or build custom landing pages) you can increase CTR to improve quality score, reduce bounce rates (which may help quality score, Google won't say) and improve conversion rates which is the reason you're advertising in the first place.

2) EARN HIGH CLICK-THROUGH RATES

Click-through rates matter above all else in the calculation of quality score. Google believes the actions of its users are the best and most important indicator of quality. It also believes past results are the best possible predictor of future behavior. So if searchers click on the ads associated with your keywords in higher proportions than the ads of your competition, you'll have excellent quality scores.

Of course, driving high click-through rates is easier said than done. But there are some basic guidelines you should follow:

♦ **Keep keywords in tightly defined ad groups**. All of the keywords in one ad group trigger the same text ads, so keywords in the group must be very narrowly focused to keep the ads highly relevant. Don't be afraid to split large ad groups into two or more smaller ones to enable a better match between keywords and text ads. In fact, the fewer the keywords per ad group the better, although we believe that in most cases 'one keyword per ad group' (a practice some advocate) is overkill.

- ◆ **Review search query lists for new positive and negative keywords**. The words users type into the search engine are called "search queries," and they're available in paid search reports. By reviewing search queries and their individual results, you can learn which keywords to add to your account as negative or positive keywords. Each new negative keyword can improve your overall click-through rate by eliminating wasted impressions. Each new phrase or exact-match keyword can improve reach, improve click-through rates, and make ad copy targeting easier and more precise.

- ◆ **Write targeted and compelling ad copy**. People click text ads that address their concerns and catch their interest. Writing great ad copy isn't easy, and it takes a lot of work to craft and test ads to find the most effective ones. But this effort is the ultimate "secret" to great quality scores.

- ◆ **Pause or delete poor performers**. Keywords with low CTRs drop your historical CTR for both the account and the associated display URLs. After organizing keywords into focused ad groups, using query mining to remove the bad and promote the good, and working hard to produce compelling ad copy, keywords that don't either earn good quality scores or deliver a profit, should be paused or deleted for the good of your business and your quality scores.

It's important to note that high click-through rates are relative. Google rates the CTR of any keyword incomparison to what it is has seen or believes is possible for that particular keyword, the searcher's particular geography, and the position in which your ad is displayed. There is no way to know if any click-through rate is a poor, good, or great just by knowing the number. A 2.5% CTR could be excellent in one case and poor in another. You'll have to gather experience, look at quality scores, and compare the performance of similar keywords in your account to get some sense of how well or poorly any keyword is doing in terms of click-through rate.

3) AVOID PENALTIES THAT SABOTAGE QUALITY SCORES

The quality score algorithms operate under the assumption that you're an honest advertiser with pure intentions . . . or at least reasonably pure intentions for a marketer :-) The system penalizes advertisers who show signs of intentionally or unintentionally disrespecting the people who search and click. These penalties can negatively impact the quality scores you'll receive for specific keywords or for all keywords in your account.

Note: Google does not refer to these negative impacts as penalties, but they clearly document the negative effect they have on quality score. The word "penalty" is applied by virtue of dramatic license.

The most common penalties are related to landing pages and site quality. Landing pages and your website as a whole play a special role in the calculation of quality score. They exist outside the technical boundaries of the AdWords system, but they have an impact on the satisfaction and experience of the people who click on paid search ads. As such, landing pages are treated differently than elements within AdWords like keywords, clicks, and ads: landing pages are primarily reviewed only to look for negative elements. If negative elements are found, then your quality scores will sink fast and far. If they're not, then—in most cases—your landing pages won't affect your quality scores.

What is Google looking for on a landing page? Anything that might be considered deceptive, suspicious, questionable, or unpleasant. Google wants to help users avoid qualitatively and quantitatively bad experiences.

Here is a *partial* list of ways to earn quality score penalties related to landing page or site quality:

♦ **Deceptive or misleading offers.** Your page or site can't promise things that are too good to be true—especially when followed by 3-point-type legalese that says you didn't really mean it. One example shown by Google included a large headline offering "10 Free DVDS" to anyone in return for signing up, but lower on the page was row after row of tiny legal type detailing impossible-to-complete requirements necessary to actually get the "free" DVDs. Offers like this can cause penalties that derail an entire AdWords account.

♦ **Pop-up or pop-under windows**. Everyone hates these. They're only used by people with no respect for their visitors. So not surprisingly, they're a total no-no in AdWords.

♦ **Slow load times**. Google measures the average page load-time performance in your region of the country (your servers), and if you are dramatically slower than that average, ding.

♦ **Misleading page redirects**. There are good and bad reasons for redirects on landing and web pages. The good ones are technical in nature and will not result in any penalty. The bad ones have to do with taking people places they didn't expect to go, and those are verboten.

♦ **Disabled browser functions**. Anything that hijacks user control of their screen or system is considered impolite and therefore not tolerated.

♦ **Duplicate or lacking original content**. If all the copy on your page was copied from another site, or worse, your site/page simply duplicates another page entirely, Google will frown.

♦ **A lack of transparency**. The landing page and site should make it clear who you are and how you treat customers and information. Specifically, AdWords looks for "about us" and "privacy policy" links.

When Google finds site quality policy violations, they can shut down your entire AdWords account. In the most extreme cases, site quality policy violations can result in an AdWords account closure and a lifetime advertiser ban from AdWords.

When Google thinks your landing page(s) are providing a poor user experience, the result is usually a landing page quality score penalty that can harm keywords associated with that landing page, or all keywords in the account. This usually won't hinder the display or position of your ads (because landing page quality score is not taken into account when deciding ad positions), but it will definitely and substantially drive up CPCs and First Page Bid Estimates.

Despite the seriousness of the risk, most advertisers need not worry about landing page penalties. These rules and retributions are designed for scammers and hardcore bad guys, not for quibbling about minor design or content choices. If you don't aggressively apply predatory practices on your landing pages, then it's unlikely you'll see many, if any, "poor" landing page designations or site policy penalties.

The exception is when Google considers your business segment or model suspicious or questionable. When Google sees a large number of advertisers in a given keyword segment run campaigns that attempt to mislead consumers or provide a questionable user experience, they sometimes chooses to suspect and pre-judge anyone who attempts to buy keywords in those same business segments. There are many markets in which Google assumes advertisers are guilty until they can prove themselves innocent—a process that isn't make clear or easy. These include "get rich quick" sites, ebooks, and many financially- and medically-related products or services.

Google also has a well-documented and reasoned distaste for anything that looks or smells like affiliate marketing, and appears to set the bar a lot higher for these sites in their pursuit of even moderate quality scores.

If your business segment or model has earned a poor reputation with Google, then it's possible (or likely) you'll have a tough time proving to them that you're an honest and reputable business. That will make it quite difficult to get good or even average quality scores for your keywords, regardless of their actual setup or performance.

THE SIMPLE PRESCRIPTION FOR GOOD QUALITY SCORES

There is and easy way to earn good to great quality scores:

1. Pick and stick with only keywords you can win.

2. Organize for relevance.

3. Optimize for click-through rates.

4. Avoid the appearance of unscrupulous behavior.

Follow these principles and your AdWords account should be filled with keywords enjoying quality scores of 7, 8, 9, and maybe even a few 10s.

What Are Good Quality Scores?

Successful AdWords accounts typically earn quality scores in the 7 to 10 range on 70% or more of their keywords. Here's how we would suggest you react to specific quality scores:

- ◆ **Celebrate keywords earning quality scores of 8, 9, or 10.**
  These scores are way above average and indicate great keyword selection, ad copy text, and account organization.

- ◆ **Relax when keywords earn quality scores of 7.**
  A visible quality score of 7 indicates that everything is probably going well for the keyword and it's earning CTRs consistent with Google's expectations and the competitive environment. The keyword will earn good if not great positions in many auctions and you'll pay a fair price per click.

- ◆ **Get to work when keywords earn quality scores of 5 or 6.**
  Quality scores of 6 or lower are generally an indication that something is wrong or could be improved. When established keywords earn quality scores of 5 or 6, you should work on improving click-through rates with better ad copy or more precise ad group organization.

- ◆ **Give up when keywords earn quality scores of 1 through 4.**
  With quality scores this low, you can certainly try to improve click-through rates using these same methods, but if CTRs and quality scores don't improve meaningfully, then you should give serious consideration to pausing or deleting low-scoring keywords. Leaving keywords with low quality scores in your account over time can negatively impact the quality scores of all your keywords by gradually lowering the historical account CTR and other universal metrics.

Do not, however, react to the quality score of any new keyword in your account until it has run for a at least few hundred and ideally 1,000 impressions. Until then you can't assume quality scores has been firmly established or stabilized. If AdWords has seen from other advertisers using your keywords they will stabilize more quickly, while truly unique keywords will take longer.

Chapter Summary

Quality score is a keyword-level rating that Google calculates to help them decide how often your ads will be shown, the position in which those ads will appear, and the price you'll be charged for each click.

It is based on a range of factors, including the historic performance of the account (primarily in terms of click-through rate), the keyword, and the text ad copy, but it can also be influenced by landing pages, business models, and other factors.

To earn high quality scores, you should:

♦ Bid only on keywords that are closely related to the products or services you're advertising.

♦ Organize your campaigns into small, focused ad groups.

♦ Write compelling ad copy that directly aligns with the subject implied in your keywords.

♦ Use landing pages which are highly relevant to the subject and free of any questionable or aggressive code or techniques that may harm or discomfort users.

The most common quality score is 7, which represents good performance and provides solid benefits. Quality scores of 6 or lower call for effort to improve the account or keyword performance. Keywords associated with scores below 5 should be paused if they can't be improved.

DISCLAIMER

Everything in this chapter is true, but it's not entirely accurate. It paints a simplified picture of quality score, leaving out many of the exceptions, side notes, and minor or major details that you'll need to know to truly optimize quality score in the messy real world.

The remainder of this book moves past this simplified picture to dig into all the gory details. We'll put quality score under the microscope and examine it from every angle: how it's calculated, the impact it has on keywords and accounts, and the steps you can take to improve quality score and thereby maximize your pay-per-click (PPC) results.

Chapter Two:
The Official Words on Quality Score

There are several places where Google shares official descriptions and comments about quality score:

- The AdWords online help system: http://goo.gl/zn2tH

- The AdWords forums: http://goo.gl/PfXMb

- The AdWords blog: http://adwords.blogspot.com/

- Conferences and events

Knowing and understanding the official Google information about quality score is critical. It may not tell you everything you want to know, but it does provide a factual base of information and help you to surmise many things that aren't fully explained. In this chapter and those that follow it, we gather the most important of the official Google statements and present them with some commentary to develop a fact-based core understanding of quality score.

> *Text quoted directly from Google is indented, italicized, and presented in dark gray type throughout the remainder of this book. Source URLs are provided at the end of each quotation so you verify this information and check for changes or clarifications.*

Google Defines Quality Score

There are several passages where Google provides a general definition and overview of quality score:

> *The AdWords system calculates a "Quality Score" for each of your keywords. It looks at a variety of factors to measure how relevant your keyword is to your ad text and to a user's search query. A keyword's Quality Score updates frequently and is closely related to its performance. In general, a high Quality Score means that your keyword will trigger ads in a higher position and at a lower cost per click (CPC).*
>
> *A Quality Score is calculated every time your keyword matches a search query—that is, every time your keyword has the potential to trigger an ad.*

Source: http://goo.gl/lAPtk

> *Quality Score is a measure of how relevant your ad, keyword, or webpage is. Quality scores help ensure that only the most relevant ads appear to users on Google and the Google Network.*
>
> *For Google and the search network, a quality score is assigned to each of your keywords. It's calculated using a variety of factors, and measures how relevant your keyword is to your ad group and to a user's search query. The higher a keyword's Quality Score, the lower its cost per clicks (CPCs) and the better its ad position.*

Source: http://goo.gl/zFmdc

WHAT IT MEANS

The message is clear and consistent: quality score measures how relevant your advertising efforts are to the people who search, and how well your keywords and ads perform. Clear and material benefits are given to those keywords that earn high quality scores.

These are important themes that will recur again and again throughout this book. Google really is trying to measure quality. It may be a subjective term and there may not be a definitive way to measure it across all of the complexity of AdWords and its huge range of advertisers, but that is the goal Google's seeking. And they believe so strongly in this ideal that they're willing to hinder advertisers who don't achieve it and assist advertisers who do.

Google Justifies Quality Score

When Google is asked why quality score is needed, here's what they say:

> *Quality Score helps ensure that only the most relevant ads appear to users on Google and the Google Network. The AdWords system works best for everybody—advertisers, users, publishers, and Google too—when the ads we display match our users' needs as closely as possible. Relevant ads tend to earn more clicks, appear in a higher position, and bring you the most success.*

Source: http://goo.gl/bxVXq

WHAT IT MEANS

At first glance, this answer sounds like marketing or public-relations "happy talk": "We're trying to deliver more relevant information and make the world a better place for everyone, blah blah blah." But actually, this answer is largely true, if somewhat incomplete and slightly disingenuous. Quality score does help everyone benefit more from AdWords. In fact, this highlights an important concept necessary to understanding quality score: the virtuous cycle.

Here's how quality score helps searchers, advertisers, and Google:

1. Quality score drives advertisers to create better campaigns.

2. These improved campaigns provide users with a better experience.

3. Searchers respond to improved ad relevance by clicking on more ads.

4. These clicks give advertisers more prospects and customers.

5. At the same time, those additional clicks drive up Google's revenue.

6. Since users are being satisfied at a higher rate, they search on Google more frequently.

7. These additional queries bring even more revenue to both advertisers and Google.

8. And because the high quality scores delivered greater click volumes at lower costs, advertiser seek out additional quality score improvements to further drive the entire process.

So quality score helps searchers get better answers, provides advertisers more qualified prospects at lower costs, and enables AdWords to become a larger and more profitable business. This is why quality score is central to the success of AdWords for everyone involved.

Google on the Factors that Influence Quality Score

The quality score formula is complicated in terms of both the number of variables it considers and the way in which the variables are defined and measured. Plus, different "versions" of quality score are applied in different circumstances.

Each of these issues will be discussed in more detail in later chapters. But here is the basic information Google offers to define the components used to calculate quality score for a given keyword:

- *The historical click-through rate (CTR) of the keyword and the matched ad on Google*
- *Your account history, which is measured by the CTR of all the ads and keywords in your account*
- *The historical CTR of the display URLs in the ad group*
- *The quality of your landing page*
- *The relevance of the keyword to the ads in its ad group*
- *The relevance of the keyword and the matched ad to the search query*
- *Your account's performance in the geographical region where the ad will be shown*
- *Other relevance factors*

Source: http://goo.gl/E6jKU

WHAT IT MEANS

This description tells us to focus on click-through rate and relevance, although it also makes clear that landing page quality, searcher geography, and "other factors" play a role. This outline tells you what to pay attention to and gives you some ideas about how to manage your account, but it isn't specific enough to tell you exactly how your campaigns need to be created, organized, or managed in order to earn high quality scores. It leaves a lot of questions unanswered.

Google on How Quality Score Impacts Your Account

Once quality score has been calculated, it impacts a number of important aspects of keyword performance in your account:

> *Quality score is used in several different ways, including influencing your keywords' actual cost per clicks (CPCs) and estimating the first page bids that you see in your account. It also partly determines if a keyword is eligible to enter the ad auction that occurs when a user enters a search query and, if it is, how high the ad will be ranked.*
>
> Source: http://goo.gl/oyG36

Google offers additional details regarding the important role quality score plays in the calculation of cost per click:

> *You always pay the lowest amount possible for the highest position you can get given your quality score and CPC bid.*
>
> *To find this amount, we divide the Ad Rank of the ad showing beneath you by your quality score, then round up to the nearest cent (we show this part of the formula as "+ $0.01" to keep things simple).*
>
> *Actual CPC = (Ad Rank to beat ÷ quality score) + $0.01*
>
> Source: http://goo.gl/e4YEF

WHAT IT MEANS

Quality score impacts every keyword in your account by:

1. Influencing each keyword's first page bid estimate

2. Determining whether or not the keyword is eligible for any ad auction, and

3. Impacting how the ad is ranked and its cost per click

It's not an overstatement to say that your success in AdWords depends on your ability to earn good quality scores.

What Google Doesn't Say about Quality Score

The descriptions and definitions listed above, plus many that are presented in subsequent chapters, aren't the only official words on quality score, but they are the most fundamental. They establish the core of what's officially known about what quality score is, how it's calculated, and how it's applied in your account.

These are reasonable, accurate, and well-intentioned statements. But they leave us with a lot of questions. And only a few of those questions are answered in subsequent Google documents. We understand there are limits to how much Google can say in some cases: for competitive reasons, to limit additional gaming of the system, and to protect their own legitimate business interests. And it is true that the vast majority of people who read the AdWords Help files are new advertisers, small advertisers, casual advertisers, or inexperienced advertisers. For the vast majority of this audience, the tone and depth of material in the AdWords Help System and even forums is excellent.

But it's clear that for serious advertisers who spend large sums of money and work tremendously hard to maximize their returns, the officially available information isn't adequate. Google's own words lay the groundwork for the mystery, uncertainty, and confusion surrounding quality score. They haven't been clear and complete enough.

Advertisers need and deserve a certain level of completeness and accuracy to make reasonable, informed, and smart business decisions. The information provided by Google describes quality score and its various aspects in broad and general terms. They offer a sense of how it works and rough examples of the steps you should take to earn good or great quality scores. But it's hard to take specific actions or make detailed decisions based on general definitions or a "sense" of how it works.

Advertisers want to know exactly (or nearly exactly) how it works. Vague or directional examples of recommended actions are inadequate. Why not provide specifics on the steps one should take to maximize results?

The tension is clear. You need more than Google has been willing to share thus far. You don't want to have to guess which setup will produce the best results, and you certainly don't want to gamble with your advertising budget. It is strange and frankly unreasonable that advertisers are asked to participate in a system—one in which large portions of marketing budgets are spent—without clear and complete access to the rules and data that drive the system. Participation is voluntary, of course, but no one understands the reality when they begin, and very few can afford an economic or political boycott of Google.

Filling in the Blanks, with Google's Help

The motivation for this book was a desire to centralize and clarify the information Google has shared publicly, and to try to fill in the blanks where they exist.

When approached, Google quickly agreed to assist our work. They were clearly aware of a desire for a deeper look into this material, and seemed pleased to find a vehicle to address these concerns in a way that could reach advanced advertisers. While working on this book, we were able to gain new insights and details about quality score, many via our discussions, interviews, and email correspondence with Google.

That is not to say that every question has been answered. We weren't able to discuss every issue with them, and in a very few cases, they declined to respond. Throughout the book, when facts aren't available or the implications or operation of something aren't known, we'll make it clear that we're sharing opinions or beliefs rather than verified facts.

Subject to Change

There is one more disclaimer. In Google's introductory description of quality score, they reserve the right to keep changing the way they calculate it:

> *While we continue to refine our quality score formulas for Google and the Search Network . . .*

It's not surprising that Google wants and needs to evolve and innovate with quality score and other aspects of their business. But it would be nice if they committed to keeping their advertisers informed of any changes which could directly impact best practices, costs, and results in a timely and complete manner.

Chapter Summary

Quality score is a metric of Google's invention. It's a secret number that pretends to be public and transparent. Google uses it to pass judgment on and rate a number of different aspects of your paid search campaigns. This rating makes value judgments about your suitability to advertise for any particular keyword at any particular time and influences your keywords and account at every step in the process.

The basics of quality score as outlined by Google are simple:

♦ Quality score measures the past and likely future performance of your keywords and the account elements that surround them.

♦ Quality Score helps Google to ensure that searchers see relevant ads, that advertisers don't flood the system with junk, and that they maximize the revenue from their available advertising inventory.

♦ Quality score determines how often your ads are shown, where they're placed, and how much you pay when they're clicked.

Quality score is presented as a simple, elegant solution to a real problem. But like many other aspects of both AdWords and Google itself, behind the simplicity lies a massively complex reality. For advanced search practitioners and advertisers spending serious money on AdWords, the information AdWords provides isn't sufficient to understand all the rules of the game or to formulate the intelligent strategies necessary to win.

The full story is enormously complicated and important, and is the subject we'll examine in great detail for the remainder of this book.

Chapter Three:
The Role of Quality Score in AdWords

In the last chapter, you learned how Google defines quality score and explains its benefits. By measuring and predicting the quality of ads, and then using this information to adjust the characteristics of their ad auctions, Google provides a better experience to searchers, advertisers, and shareholders.

But quality score has other advantages for Google, too. It helps them shape the way individual advertisers interact with AdWords. Some of these implications may be unintentional, but they're all useful to Google and important for advertisers to understand.

1. **Quality Score Encourages Good Advertisers.** The benefits of high quality scores act as a kind of "preferred customer program" to reward advertisers who produce good or great CTRs while avoiding elements or actions that can limit quality scores.

2. **Quality Score Discourages Bad Advertisers.** The incremental costs and lost opportunity suffered due to poor quality scores provide a "bozo filter" that limits or prevents undesirable ads and advertisers.

3. **Quality Score Confuses Almost All Advertisers.** To most AdWords customers, quality score is a "secret sauce" that limits their understanding of how and why keywords and ads behave as they do, and therefore stifles effort and results.

This chapter examines each of these impacts of quality score.

Quality Score as Preferred Customer Program

Google wants to help advertisers who have proven their ability to get high CTRs on specific keywords and in general across their account. These advertisers buy more clicks from Google, spend a lot of money on an ongoing basis, and demonstrate that they know how to build, manage, and grow their accounts while satisfying searchers. Google wants to keep them happy and active.

By offering a system whereby these advertisers earn high quality scores, both across their accounts and on specific keywords, Google rewards them with serious benefits including more impressions and lower prices. How large are these advantages? It's impossible to say for sure. It's reasonable to assume that keywords earning the very best quality scores generate many times the impression volume at much lower total cost than keywords that earn mediocre quality scores.

In addition, advertisers who prove they know how to earn the good or great quality scores get the benefit of the doubt in the form of higher starting scores when they add new keywords, test new text ads, or even start advertising in new categories.

Quality Score as a Bozo Filter

At the other end of the spectrum, AdWords needs a way of controlling ineffective advertisers, or those who are somehow trying to game the system in a way that harms searchers or Google itself.

Accidental Bozos

At one extreme are those who get into AdWords with dreams or delusions of a quick or easy buck and flood the system with their own inexperience. They may in fact be new and naïve, or they may be long-time advertisers who somehow manage to remain incompetent. In either case, they do nearly everything wrong: their campaigns have sloppy keyword selection, bad text ads, poor organization, and most likely lousy landing pages with undifferentiated or even questionable offers.

But they have money to spend and are often willing to bid somewhat or entirely irrationally. If quality score didn't exist, nothing would throttle back the impact of these advertisers. Their poor campaign execution and their ad dollars would allow their inexperience to pollute the system and distort the reasonable efforts of better advertisers.

To these advertisers, quality score acts like a handicapping system, preventing damage to other participants and the system itself. New advertisers have to earn and prove their way onto a level playing field. If they can't make it, they're discouraged or prevented from distorting the experience and performance of established and proven advertisers.

Intentional Bozos

At the other extreme are professional internet scammers. They're the exact opposite of the new and inexperienced; they're far more sophisticated than the average AdWords advertiser. The trouble is they're up to no good— attempting to sell disreputable products or services, arbitrage click costs, or trick or swindle people in one way or another.

They tend to move fast, picking up on hot trends or morphing hundreds of times within the bounds of a long-running shady domain. They pick keywords, create landing pages, test relentlessly, make some money, and move on to the next area.

In this area, quality score is a consumer protection service. It penalizes pages that use deceptive practices or language, fail to make proper disclosures, or show other signs of real or potentially nefarious activities. The "account history" component of quality score acts a little like a "three strikes and you're out" law; a poor history diminishes the chance (or at least increases the cost) of new and future successes. The "business model" and "business segment" reviews put extra hurdles in front of anyone who tries to advertise in any area where troublemakers have been known to congregate.

Paying the Bozo Tax

When low quality scores are assigned to accidental or intentional bozos, their ads appear less frequently, in lower positions, and at higher costs. But except in rare cases, these penalties don't prevent ads from appearing altogether. If advertisers are willing to compensate for low quality scores with higher bids (sometimes significantly higher), then their keywords will get into auctions and their ads can even appear in high positions.

Google walks a fine line between controlling bad advertisers and sabotaging their own revenues. Bad quality scores produce extra money for Google in the short run because they drive up CPCs. They drive even more revenue when advertisers raise bids in reaction to lower quality scores. Many advertisers with low quality scores caused by poor execution or efforts to game the system will dramatically overpay for long periods of time.

But eventually, as quality scores continue to deteriorate, it can become difficult for these advertisers to get many impressions or clicks. Advertisers may eventually decide it's not worth the increased costs and stop spending entirely. For Google, these "lost" advertising dollars are the price they pay to keep the overall experience for searchers positive.

On the other hand, many advertisers do learn from poor quality scores and take the steps necessary to improve them. In such cases, quality score can be frustrating, but it is ultimately forgiving.

It's easy to say that the increased revenue Google earns from low quality scores are an unfair "windfall profit." If their goal is really just a better search experience, then shouldn't something else happen with the extra CPCs they're getting from low quality score advertisers? How about a rebate to advertisers in those auctions with quality scores of 7 or higher?

Our contention is that the onus is mostly on those low quality score advertisers. Low quality scores are designed to be a motivator: to incite advertisers to improve click-through rates or stop advertising on keywords that aren't effective or efficient. Otherwise, the only choice is to pay the bozo tax, and if you do that, Google will gladly collect it.

Quality Score as Secret Sauce

The fact that quality score has a huge impact on your advertising success and yet you don't have full visibility into its calculation and application is an advantage to Google. By creating uncertainty and confusion among advertisers, even if unintentionally, quality score limits the ability of advertisers to take deliberate action to improve their results.

Advertisers want transparency, and the AdWords system appears transparent; you pick the keywords, set the budget, write your ads, and define your bids. You're shown the CTR and CPC and can track your conversion rates. But in reality the system is quite opaque because mixed throughout—lightly but liberally—is quality score. And quality score has a number of important effects that reduce transparency:

♦ **You don't know how many advertising opportunities you miss**. Each keyword in an AdWords account is an attempt to reach a certain audience or group of people. But before your ads can be shown to some of these people, quality score renders the keywords ineligible for the auctions triggered by certain related search queries. AdWords doesn't report on these missed opportunities either in general (with an impression share–like statistic) or in detail (with a list of queries where your keyword was ruled ineligible). Your view of the potential surrounding any keyword and the cost of a poor quality score is entirely obscured.

Even when a keyword enters an auction, it may then fail to earn an impression due ad rank (ad rank = bid x quality score). In this case, the Impression Share metric provides a little feedback, but only for the rollup of every keyword in an entire campaign. No detailed reporting informs you of which search query opportunities were missed. You're left with an imprecise, and probably inaccurate, view of the landscape of searchers you're trying to target and reach. It's like drilling for oil and missing a huge pool by only a few feet without knowing that you're close to a major discovery. If you could see what you're missing, then you could take action to capture it.

♦ **You don't know if bid or quality score is constraining your position.** The fact that position is determined by ad rank (bid x quality score) is clear, but without any visibility into your competitors' bids and quality scores (and assuming you're doing your best to earn good quality scores), it's hard not to think that increasing bid is the only practical way to improve ad position.

If AdWords displayed some relative indicator of quality score performance—for instance, "This quality score is 1.3 points lower than the average of the ads in the top 3 positions," or "This quality score is 1.3 points lower than the highest quality score currently earned for this keyword"—the you could better prioritize your efforts to improve quality score without feeling like any significant increases are impossible.

Interestingly, the AdWords Bid Simulator provides insight (for high volume keywords) into the potential of CPC increases to earn better positions and improve click volume. A similar tool for quality score would be wonderful.

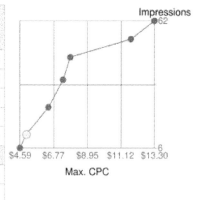

| Bid simulator: [ppc bid management software] | | | ■ |

Simulation based on performance from May 16, 2011 to May 22, 2011
These estimates do not guarantee similar results in the future. Learn more

Max. CPC	Estimated Impr.	Estimated Top Impr. ⑦
◎ $13.30	62	10
◎ $11.80	54	6
◎ $7.84	46	2
◎ $7.38	36	--
◎ $6.44	24	--
◉ $5.00 (current)	12	--
◎ $4.59	6	--
◎ Use a different bid: $ _____		

♦ **The relationship between max CPC and average CPC is unclear.**
Setting or changing maximum CPC (increasing or decreasing a
bid) has only an indirect impact on the actual CPC for a keyword
because of the way costs are calculated. Bid is used along with
quality score to calculate ad rank and decide position, but the
CPC for any click is based on the next highest advertiser's ad rank
divided by your keyword's quality score. The result is that your bid
will not always reflect your CPC. For instance, if you raise your bid
by $1.00, sometimes your average CPC will rise by $0.90, and other
times by only $0.10.

The Bid Simulator provides great insights for the keywords for
which it's available, but that's only a small percentage of the
keywords in most accounts.

Another confusing factor is that as you raise your bid for any non-
exact match keyword it will become eligible for additional search
query auctions, and often the average position and average CPC for
these incremental queries will be higher than the majority of the
existing ones. There is no way to identify these "extra" auctions.

At the end of the day, the complex interaction of your bid, your
quality score, your ad rank, competitive advertisers' actions, search
query eligibility, and the actual CPC calculation is a complicated
black box. You can see what goes in and what comes out but have
no idea why. Many of these factors vary for each search query but
the associated metrics are reported only as averages, —which makes
the mystery even deeper.

♦ **You don't know how much any click costs.** There is a reason
AdWords reports the "average CPC" for every keyword. Unless a
keyword gets only a single click in a full day, you never know what
any individual click really cost. Since CPC calculations are based
on search query competition and quality scores, user geography, and
other factors, there could be—and is likely—great variation in how
much the different clicks for a single keyword cost. Are you paying
the most for the most valuable queries and the least for the least
valuable ones? You don't know.

Of course, it's likely that full transparency would radically change and probably kill the system. The current fuzziness keeps expectations (and tempers) in check, but it limits advertiser visibility and control.

It appears that Google is happy to have advertisers *optimize*, which results in increased volume and lower prices. But they stop short of enabling you to produce results which are *optimal*; advertisers don't have the data to figure out how *exactly* to get the highest number of qualified clicks for the lowest price.

Quality score is an innovation that improves the overall AdWords experience for all involved. But a byproduct of the way it's calculated, and of the data that is and isn't shared, is that quality score obscures a lot about the performance of your AdWords account.

Addressing Concerns without Answering Questions

Quality score also helps Google by allowing them to respond to questions and complaints without really answering the questions being asked. For example: Suppose you're dissatisfied with how frequently your ads are run, their average position, or the price you're paying per click. On any other advertising or marketing platform, you'd expect to have a serious conversation with your vendor, including a detailed explanation of why your ad wasn't run, why it was placed where it was, or how your price was calculated.

But on AdWords, the conversation will both take place and end very differently. The answer, almost certainly, is simply, "Your keywords didn't earn a high enough quality score. If you can improve your quality score, the system will show your ad more frequently, in higher positions, and possibly at lower prices."

To the untrained eye, this sounds reasonable. But as an advertiser spending money on the AdWords network, it really isn't. They're telling you to do better without telling you *how* to do better. They're telling you to do better without being willing to share the metrics you need to track your progress or test different improvement efforts. In the parlance of web analytics, they're providing mere data rather than actionable insight.

Imagine Google's rules applied in another situation: Suppose your home mortgage had a similar variable pricing component based on the "quality score" of your home for the prior month determined by attributes such as the attractiveness of your yard, the cleanliness of your home, the status of your neighborhood, and "other desirability factors." Would it bother you when you opened that bill each month that you weren't allowed to see your score on any of these attributes and weren't provided any specific information about the way they were judged or calculated or what actions would improve them? Can you imagine signing a mortgage with those terms and conditions? Of course not; nobody would.

Yet millions of advertisers agree to participate on a marketing platform with essentially these very same terms and conditions.

Better yet, imagine yourself the owner of a company with a large national client base. Pretend that your customers agreed to buy your service on a regular ongoing basis, despite the fact that you change the particulars of the service you provide to them and the amount you charge them on a regular basis. And suppose that you're allowed to make pricing changes based on proprietary formulas of which your customers have only limited knowledge and no forewarning of the outcome.

Wouldn't that be great? Yes.

Perhaps we have a new definition of the verb "to Google"?

Chapter Summary

Quality Score is the special ingredient that makes AdWords work. It feeds the good, starves the bad, and helps Google create an environment that enables the whole system to flourish. The devil, of course, is in the details.

Quality score helps "good advertisers." Those who are lucky or skilled enough to buy keywords that are clicked at high absolute rates, and particularly those with ads clicked at high rates relative to competitors' ads (due to brand awareness or copywriting prowess), tend to do well in the quality score system. Advertisers who aren't skilled in the process or who display less than the best of intentions toward their visitors don't fare so well under the pressure of quality score. The meritocratic approach of the system is great and appropriate, although it can be tough on those who find themselves stuck in the second bucket and can't quite figure out how to move into the first.

As described earlier, the existence of quality score benefits advertisers, searchers, and Google themselves. But these benefits are not, and probably could not be, split perfectly equally among these three. Since one of the players happens to be making all the rules, holding all the cards, and keeping some of the rules and the cards secret, it's not surprising that this player gains some unique and distinct advantages.

Advertisers must work to maximize their own results, both by understanding the details of quality score well enough to earn good scores and gain as much benefit as possible, and by continuing to pressure Google to increase the transparency of their platform.

Chapter Four:
Which Quality Score?

Before moving too much further, we should examine one of the clearest distinctions between the rather simple notion of quality score as it is commonly and officially described, and the more complex reality of quality score: the question of which quality score is being discussed at any given time.

If you casually read the official AdWords information about quality score, hear people discuss it, or even read the first few chapters of this book, you could easily get the impression that quality score is a single metric and always an attribute of individual keywords. Yet neither of these is true.

There are several different measures called "quality score," and a single keyword can earn many different quality scores.

The fact that the same name is applied interchangeably to different things is one of the chief reasons why quality score is so confusing. In this chapter, we'll demystify the various metrics and measures referred to as quality score.

The Quality Scores

There are three primary versions of quality score, and several additional "component" quality scores that are frequently referred to in quality score discussions. As explained below, each version differs in what it measures and how it is used.

Qual. score
--
10/10
10/10
8/10
7/10
7/10

♦ **Visible quality score**: The keyword-level metric reported in AdWords as a number between 1 and 10 is what most people think of when they read or hear the name quality score. This version is designed to be an easy-to-use approximation of the quality score earned by each keyword. It does not reflect many of the factors considered in the calculation of other quality score versions, and it has no impact beyond providing feedback to advertisers and paid search managers.

♦ **Quality score for ad rank**: This is the quality score number used to decide if a particular keyword is eligible for an auction, and if the keyword is eligible then it is used to calculate the keyword's ad rank, which determines the position in which the ad will appear. This version is calculated in real-time after someone executes a search, and considers factors such as the search query and user geography that do not impact visible quality score.

♦ **Quality score for CPC**: The quality score for ad rank is adjusted to take into account landing page and other factors not used in that version to create this version of quality score. This is then used to calculate the cost per click for a specific text ad in a given auction.

♦ **Component quality scores**: The historic performance of many account elements that are used in the calculation of the three versions of quality score described above, are themselves often referred to as quality scores. Examples include text ad quality score, landing page quality score, and even account quality score.

The differences between visible quality score and the quality scores used for ad rank and CPC are the most important to understand because the former creates the impression that it's given you the information needed to manage the results produced by the later – but in many cases it does not. For example, suppose you read a AdWords help file that says 'quality score considers the relevance of your search queries to your keywords' and so you decide to review the performance of search queries for some of the keywords that have low quality scores in your account. But actually the visible quality score that drove your action isn't affected by most of the search queries in that report. It's easy to get frustrated or confused.

The Details of Visible Quality Score

The quality score metric AdWords displays in the interface alongside each individual keyword is an approximation designed to represent the many different quality scores a keyword earns in the different search auctions for which it is eligible. This number *is not* the quality score number used in the calculations that determine your position or CPC. In this book, we call this number the "visible quality score."

Google admits that visible quality score is not the number they use in ad rank or CPC calculations:

> *Please note that the Quality Score detail is not the same as the numeric quality multiplier we use when calculating Ad Rank or cost per click (CPC). The Quality Score detail scale does not change the way that Quality Score is calculated or considered.*

> Source: http://goo.gl/ioiIS

Visible quality score serves the same purpose for PPC as the PageRank number shown in the Google Toolbar does for SEO: it gives you an idea of the number Google is using behind the scenes. But it is not that number.

How Visible Quality Score Is Unique

There are at least six ways that visible quality score differs from the quality score AdWords uses to calculate eligibility, position, cost, and first page bid estimates:

♦ **Visible quality score is only updated once per day, at most.** The number reported as visible quality score represents a summary of recent performance for that keyword. Quality scores for ad rank and CPC, by contrast, are calculated and adjusted in real time, as a search takes place, using the most complete data available.

> *Search advertising is a dynamic, evolving marketplace, and the quality score of your keywords can fluctuate. We continually monitor the performance of all ads, keywords, and landing pages in our system to reward high quality ads and encourage advertisers to improve low quality ads.*

Source: http://goo.gl/lCpA8

> *Quality Score will now be more accurate because it will be calculated at the time of each search query . . .*

Source: http://goo.gl/TuSsR

♦ **Visible quality score does not consider user geography.** Visible quality score is calculated based on all users in all geographies of all versions of a keyword. Quality scores for ad rank and CPC, on the other hand, consider the geographic location of the searcher.

♦ **Visible quality considers only search queries identical to the keyword.** The visible quality score of any keyword in your account is based only on the performance of that keyword for those times when it was matched with search queries identical to the keyword itself. Keywords with broad or phrase match types will enter and win auctions for all kinds of search queries other than those identical to the keyword, but the CTRs from those impressions are not used in the calculation of visible quality score.

Quality Score is calculated based on keyword performance only when a keyword perfectly matches a search query.

Source: http://goo.gl/xmrnd

This is not to say that quality score is only calculated for exact match keywords. It is actually calculated for the combined performance of all match type versions of any keyword in the account, but based upon only the CTR of search queries that are identical to the keyword.

Match type does not directly impact quality score. If you were to add the same keyword three times to your ad group, each with a different match type, they would all have the same quality score. This means that identical keywords in your ad group will have the same first page bid estimates, regardless of their match types.

Source: http://goo.gl/9W5e3

The CTRs of non-identical search queries do, however, impact the quality scores for ad rank and CPC. But they're considered in the "relevance" portion of the quality score calculation, as described later in this chapter. The quality score management implications of the treatment of search queries that are not identical to your keywords is discussed in *Chapter Eleven: Everyday Quality Score Management*.

♦ **Visible quality score aggregates the performance of all text ads.** Most keywords trigger various ads from their ad group, and each different ad results in a different click-through rate. Visible quality score uses the combined performance of all the ad versions triggered by that keyword. Quality score for ad rank and CPC consider only the performance history of the specific text ad being used with the keyword in that particular instance.

If there are three ads in the ad group holding a keyword, and two of them have a 3% CTR when shown with that keyword and one of them has a 6% CTR when shown with that keyword, then the quality score of that keyword will be higher when paired with one of the better-performing text ads. So even excluding other factors, each keyword has as many different quality scores for ad rank as the number of text ads in the ad group. But each keyword has only one visible quality score, which essentially averages these results.

♦ **Visible quality score is identical for all instances of a keyword.** If a keyword appears multiple times in your account, with different match types or in any number of campaigns with custom geo-targeting settings, each version of the keyword will always display the same visible quality score. The combined performance of all versions—for identical search queries and regardless of user geography, as explained above—is considered in this calculation. Quality score for ad rank and CPC considers the search queries, user geography, and associated ad copy in all calculations.

Note that plural or other unique variations of a keyword are each considered separately and earn their own unique quality scores.

♦ **Visible quality score is an integer between 1 and 10.** While Google uses the the numbers 1 through 10 to report on visible quality score, these are not the numbers, or the numeric range, used by quality score for ad rank or CPC.

We don't know exactly what numbers Google uses in those other quality scores, but it's likely they use numbers with a broader range than 1 to 10 (some of their help files show quality score numbers of 40, for example). There have also been reports that inside the AdWords system, all quality scores are decimals between 0 and 1. It's also almost certain that Google calculates quality score as a real and not a whole number. The quality score used to calculate the ad rank of a keyword/ad combo might be 16.29498 or .01229498.

NOTE: Throughout this book, we will continue to use the visible quality score numbers of 1 to 10 in most examples and discussions.

As you can see, there are significant differences between visible quality score and the quality scores that drive ad rank and CPC. Visible quality score is a useful metric in that it gives you an idea of how each keyword in your account is performing in both absolute terms and relative to your other keywords. And the reality is that it's the only summary information available to indicate even approximately what quality scores your keywords are earning.

But as you dive deeper into the complexities of quality score management and troubleshooting, it helps to remember that it's only approximation of your quality score. You'll often need to look past the visible quality score and consider the factors that drive quality score for ad rank and CPC in order to maximize your results.

The Component Quality Scores

In the calculation of visible quality score and quality score for ad rank or CPC, the AdWords system uses historical performance ratings and scores they've calculated or assigned to various components of your account. Many of these are referred to as "quality scores" in documents or discussions.

Here are the ones you may come across:

- **Landing Page Quality Score.** Each landing page is assessed and given what may be a pass/fail quality grade based on a range of factors as described in *Chapter 5: How Quality Score Is Calculated*. This quality score is then used as a component within the calculation of the quality score for CPC and the First Page Bid Estimate.

- **Account Quality Score.** The historic CTR of the account is considered as part of the ad rank quality score calculation, and the domain-level CTR history of target URLs is a factor, and these are sometimes referred to as the "account quality score." It isn't clear how either element are applied, but in most cases they should play a larger role in the initial quality score calculations for new keywords and diminish in influence as the keyword builds up more direct CTR history.

♦ **Text-Ad Quality Score.** The phrase "ad quality" is sometimes used, but it's not clear if or how the overall CTR history of an ad across different keywords is actually applied. It may be used when calculating the quality score for a new keyword that does not yet have sufficient impression or click history, or the phrase may just be a reference to the broader concept of better AdWords results or user experience and not something specifically used within quality score.

Quality Score on Google and Beyond

Both the data considered in the calculation of quality score and the formula used to calculate quality score depend upon the network where ads are running. Google differentiates between searches done on Google.com, those done on major partner sites such as AOL or Comcast, and those that take place on their widely distributed Display Network.

♦ **Search Network Quality Score.** All quality score calculations for searches that take place on Google.com or in the Google Toolbar are made separately based on different data than the quality score calculations that apply when keywords appear on the Google Search Network (sites outside of Google.com that display Google search results). Visible quality score in AdWords reflects only performance on Google.com and in the Google Toolbar.

♦ **Display Network (Content Network) Quality Score.** Keywords and placements running on the Google Display Network (formerly the Content Network) are subject to an entirely different set of quality score calculations and effects than those that take place on Google.com.

Chapter Summary

Quality score is a broad concept, and the term is used to represent a number of different measures and metrics that AdWords uses to track and predict performance and impact your advertising efforts. Google itself uses the phrase to refer to different metrics that are calculated and applied in different ways. As a paid search manager, you must understand quality score well enough to know which version is being referenced in any given discussion.

There are several frequently discussed versions of quality score:

- **Visible quality score** is the most commonly used and referenced version. This is the number reported on a daily basis for each keyword in your account. This score acts as the representative or approximation for two more precise and impactful versions of quality score: quality score for ad rank and quality score for CPC.

- **Quality score for ad rank** is calculated at the time of each search and considers detailed performance history relative to the user's search query, geographic location, and other factors.

- **Quality score for CPC** builds on quality score for ad rank, additionally taking into account landing page quality.

The term "quality score" is also sometimes used in relation to measured components within your account, such as landing pages and text ads.

All quality score numbers that apply to searches and keywords on Google itself are distinct from those calculated for and applied to ads run on Google's partner sites (such as AOL or Comcast), blogs, and other sites that are part of the Google Display Network. Performance or results from these other advertising channels have no impact on any quality score calculation for Google.com. Different versions of quality score are calculated and applied to those searches.

Part II:
Understanding Quality Score

Chapter Five:
How Quality Score Is Calculated

The $64,000 question for advertisers and paid search managers is: "How does Google determine quality score?"

There isn't a simple answer to this question, both because the formula is secret and because they vary the calculation based on the type of information available to them at the time. All we can do is understand the factors that influence quality score and the situations in which specific factors are likely to have more or less weight.

Google provides a relatively simple bullet list of the influential factors, but this chapter takes a detailed look at each of them. We'll look at what each factor is measuring and discuss the real-world methods and implications of controlling and optimizing those aspects of your account.

The Factors that Influence Quality Score

The AdWords help files list eight factors when describing how quality score is calculated. Breaking these down by type, we find three factors related to CTR, three related to relevance, one related to landing pages, and one related to the geographic location of the searcher.

- ◆ Click-through Rate Factors
    - ◆ The historical click-through rate (CTR) of the keyword and the matched ad on Google
    - ◆ Your account history, which is measured by the CTR of all the ads and keywords in your account
    - ◆ The historical CTR of the display URLs in the ad group
- ◆ Relevance Factors
    - ◆ The relevance of the keyword to the ads in its ad group
    - ◆ The relevance of the keyword and the matched ad to the search query
    - ◆ Other relevance factors
- ◆ Landing Page Factors
    - ◆ The quality of your landing page
- ◆ Geographic Factors
    - ◆ Account performance in the geographical region where the ad will be shown

Below we take a detailed look at each of these components.

Factor #1: Click-through Rate

When someone clicks on your ad, they're indicating that it interests them, giving you the chance to earn a customer, and helping Google make money. It's no wonder that click-through rate is the driving factor in quality score.

As Google says:

> *Click-through rate (CTR) is the most significant component of quality score because it directly indicates which ads are most relevant to our searchers.*
>
> Source: http://goo.gl/ijxUf

Google believes clicks *are* quality, and nothing predicts the future success of a keyword like its past success. They've referred to this method of measuring relevance as the "wisdom of the crowd." Any ad that appears in search results and gets a lot of clicks is deemed relevant to that search and of high quality.

MEET THE CLICK-THROUGH RATES

While it makes sense that the historical click-through rate of the keyword is the first (and largest) factor in quality score, you may be surprised to learn that the CTR metric reported in AdWords (and most third-party tools) *is not* the version of CTR that's used in the calculation of quality score. This means that reviewing the click-through rate AdWords provides for any particular keyword may not help you understand why that keyword is earning a given quality score.

The keyword-level CTR metric in AdWords reports on the total click-through rate for the keyword based on all of its impressions against all search queries, in all geographies, and as matched to all text ads in the ad group. As in many other cases, AdWords is sharing an average, when as a serious paid search manager, you'd really rather be able to see the raw data.

Instead of using the average CTR of the keyword, Google relies on four different and very specific versions of CTR to calculate quality score:

♦ The historical CTR of the keyword and matched ad on Google

♦ The historical CTR of the account

♦ The historical CTR of the display URLs in your ad group

♦ Performance (CTR) in the geography where the ad is shown

The following sections explore each of these CTR measures in detail.

HISTORICAL CTR OF THE KEYWORD AND MATCHED AD

It's not the CTR of the keyword itself that drives quality score, but the CTR of keyword + ad copy combinations. This is an important distinction.

Most ad groups include two or more variations, and as you know, different ads earn different click-through rates. Each unique keyword + ad combination therefore results in a different quality score. As each ad gets its turn to enter auctions the quality score for that keyword + ad combination will be used in the eligibility calculation that determines whether or not the ad earns a slot and, if so, its position and price.

Suppose you had an ad group called "baseball bats" that included the keyword "little league approved bat" and had two running text ads set to "Rotate".

If the keyword has historically earned at 2.2% CTR when paired with the "Little League Bats" ad copy, but only a 1.1% CTR when paired with the "Approved Bats for Kids" ad copy, then every time "Approved Bats for Kids" is used along with the keyword in an action, it will earn a lower quality score than it does when "Little League Bats" is used.

This is why you must aggressively manage the text ads in your ad groups in order to maximize quality score and campaign success. Whenever

Little League Bats
Visit us for all your batting needs
Free shipping and no return hassles
www.lilleaguebats.com/specials

Approved Bats for Kids
Hit Harder Brand Little League Bats
Free shipping and no return hassles
www.lilleaguebats.com/specials

one ad in an ad group is receiving a lower CTR than the other ads in that ad group, it impacts the quality score of every keyword it's paired with every time it's used. In addition to impacting performance results, over time this lower-performing ad copy drags down the average visible quality score for all the keywords in that ad group.

Given the huge impact ad copy has on click-through rates, it's not surprising that Google wants to judge keyword and ad combinations. Doing so allows them to reward good ads with a high quality score and discourage less productive ads via a low quality score.

Unfortunately, it's not easy to manage the CTR of keyword + ad copy combinations. CTR is not reported for these pairs in the standard AdWords interface or via the AdWords API. Keyword-level CTR as reported in AdWords is a weighted average of the CTR of that keyword across all running text ads. The CTR reported for each text ad is an average CTR of that ad when matched with all the different keywords in the ad group. So you can see how a keyword does across all the ads, or how an ad does across all the keywords, but you can't see the CTR of any keyword-ad pair.

You can, however, see CTRs for keyword-ad pairs in a downloaded report from the Ads tab in AdWords:

1. Click the Ads tab.

2. Click the Download Report button.

3. Click +Add Segment and select "Keyword/ Placement."

4. Click the Create button.

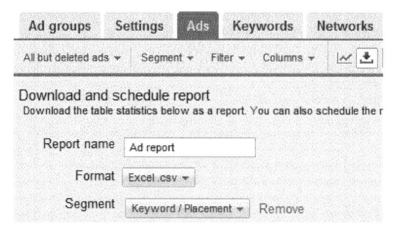

What about New or Modified Text Ads?

The fact that each ad copy version influences quality score may make you worry about creating new ads or editing existing ad copy, but have no fear.

When new or modified ads are introduced into an ad group, Google assumes they'll get an average CTR based on the other ads in that ad group until the ad builds up some history of its own. It isn't clear if they use the average CTR of only the currently running ads, or factor in the average CTR of recently run ads. But in any case, they don't begin with the assumption of 0% CTR, so there is no danger or damage (in terms of quality score) in writing and testing new ad copy. In fact, you should do it as much as possible.

Historical CTR of the Account

The historical CTR of your AdWords account is like your lifetime batting average. It tells Google if you're a skilled advertiser or an unskilled one. Google uses this information to decide whether to give you the benefit of the doubt or to assume that you'll probably somehow disappoint them, every time you make a change to your account.

Google has not disclosed the specific way in which they use historical account-level data. Instead, they've said that like other factors, different amounts of historical data are used based on how confident (or not) they are about the expected performance of a given keyword or ad. Past performance never really goes away, but it does have a diminishing impact over time in the case of most keywords and ads.

It is possible but unlikely that a simple average lifetime CTR is used in the quality score calculation. There is anecdotal evidence that very old AdWords accounts (those that have been active for five-plus years) that have had large and productive budgets for many years get an important boost from this history. Some people even buy old discarded AdWords accounts to get this magic foundation on which to build their own accounts. Google, however, claims this deep history should not provide undue advantages.

Similarly, accounts that were in poor shape and left that way for many months or a few years appear to suffer near permanent and perhaps irrecoverable damage. Even the advisors in the AdWords help forums have been known to tell people who inherit management of accounts with bad histories to scrap them and start over in brand new AdWords accounts. (See *Chapter Ten: Dealing with Disaster* for more details)

Since the historical CTR of your account impacts your quality score, you will want to track it over time. Well, you're in luck; other than the ad-hoc keyword-to-ad copy reporting mentioned above, this is the only metric used in the calculation of quality score that is actually reported on in the AdWords interface. To see your account's historical CTR:

1. Go to the AdWords Home tab.

2. In the Campaign Performance area, choose "All Time" as the date range and "CTR" as the metric.

The fact that the historical CTR of the account is used in the calculation of quality scores has all kinds of interesting implications. It means that anything you do in your account can affect performance across the account in the immediate and the distant future.

The Myth of Ad-Group Quality Score

It's worth noting that neither ad group– or campaign-level CTRs are used in the calculation of quality score. The idea of ad group– and campaign-level CTR or quality score is frequently discussed in blogs, tweets, and forums, but Google says these are not tracked or considered.

The way you choose to organize keywords into ad groups impacts your quality scores by defining the relationship (and therefore relevance) between search queries, keywords, and ad copy, which impacts click-through rates. Organization matters, but not because of ad group– or campaign-level quality scores or CTR.

HISTORICAL CTR OF DISPLAY URLS

This is interesting and clever—AdWords tracks and considers the historical CTR of each display URL you use in your text ads as part of the quality score calculation. And it's an element that is rarely, if ever, discussed as a tool for quality score management.

There are a large number of text ads in almost all AdWords accounts, but most advertisers use a fairly small number of distinct display URLs. Some only use one: every ad includes the website URL as the display URL.

Those advertisers who do vary their target URLs often use them in a categorical way, such as having all the dog food keywords use a URL that ends in "/dogfood." Other times, target URLs are used to reinforce the topic keyword in some way, such as by appending the specific product name to the URL (as in "/puppychow").

Round Rubber Balls
Feel great in your hands
Bounce remarkably well too
rubberballs.com/discounts

Round Rubber Balls
Feel great in your hands
Bounce remarkably well too
rubberballs.com

Round Rubber Balls
Feel great in your hands
Bounce remarkably well too
round.rubberballs.com

Round Rubber Balls
Feel great in your hands
Bounce remarkably well too
www.rubberballs.com/round

Round Rubber Balls
Feel great in your hands
Bounce remarkably well too
www.rubberballs.com

By tracking the CTR history of each display URL, Google learns how good you are at marketing a particular category, product, or perhaps webpage. They then use this information—correctly or not—to decide if you should get an advantage, or at least the chance to prove yourself when you try to market that same thing with a new keyword or text ad.

The fact that Google tracks and takes the performance of display ULRs into account means that display URLs should be managed with some degree of intentionality. You should think about which ones to use for which ad groups, and keep in mind how well any given URL has done in the past.

Actively managing display URLs is not an easy task for several reasons, the main one being that it's virtually impossible to keep track of the CTR history for each display URL used in your ads. AdWords does not provide this reporting, and you would need to be amazingly diligent to track these numbers yourself.

Want to try it? Here are the general steps you'll need to take:

1. Export a text ad performance report.

2. Group the available rows by display URL.

3. Recalculate weighted averages for the CTRs.

4. Track them over time and try to see their influence on quality scores.

Yikes.

Geographical Performance

The performance of your account in the geographical area where searchers are located is the final CTR-related factor. Your account may see high click-through rates from people living in the Pacific Northwest, for example, but very low CTRs from Gulf Coast searchers. Google considers this performance and lowers your quality score (and thereby reduces impressions and position and increases CPC) for searchers who live in areas less likely to click on your ads.

This geographic consideration is largely at the account level rather than the keyword level. The overall performance of your account in a geographic region will impact the quality score of all individual keywords.

> *Quality Score Factors:*
> *Your account's performance in the geographical region where the ad will be shown . . .*
>
> Source: http://goo.gl/P75FH

This would suggest that if the majority of your account does poorly in a particular geography where a few keywords or ad groups perform very well, quality scores for both the good and the bad performers would suffer in that geography. In interviews conducted for this book, however, Google said that individual keywords that get good CTRs in areas where the rest of the account performs poorly should be able to earn good quality scores. We suspect that the query-specific relevance rating in effect overcomes the broader account-wide performance in those cases.

Remember that geographic impact is not reflected in visible quality score. It is instead applied during the real-time calculation of quality score for ad rank. This means that your quality scores for ad rank and CPC may be significantly lower or higher than visible quality score suggests, depending on the geographic location of the searcher.

OTHER CTR FACTORS

The fact that AdWords is looking at the four specialized versions of CTR described above isn't the only complexity surrounding how click-through rate impacts quality score. CTR is also normalized for position; filtered based on the ad network and platform; and calculated (at least for display purposes) without regard for match type, geography, or search query variations.

♦ CTR is normalized for position in the quality score calculation. Since ads running in higher positions get higher click-through rates, you might expect the keyword/ad combinations shown in higher positions to get higher quality scores.

But Google says they won't, because they normalize CTR by position before calculating quality score. In other words, they take the position into account and reverse the boost from a high position or the drag from a low one.

> *Ads in high positions typically earn better CTR than those in low positions, because ads in high positions are more visible to searchers. To calculate the most accurate quality scores, it's important that the influence of ad position on CTR be taken into account and removed from the quality score.*
>
> *Your keywords should get the quality score they deserve regardless of the position in which they run.*
>
> Source: http://goo.gl/VqsWJ

Note: Independent tests have shown that the normalization algorithms may not be perfect, and Google representatives have admitted as much. So keywords running in higher positions *may* in fact get a slight quality score advantage. A number of advertisers— including those generally in the know on PPC best practices—very commonly "prime the pump" by over-bidding on new keywords to get higher positions when they first add the keywords to their accounts. Once good or great quality scores are established, they may then reduce their bids to more "return justified" levels.

♦ Only the CTR for impressions on Google.com are used to calculate quality scores for keywords when ads are running on Google.com. Through your AdWords account, you can run ads on Google.com, on search partner sites such as AOL, in mobile search results, and/ or on sites across the internet that participate in Google's Display Network. Google recognizes that click-through rates in these other channels are different than they are on Google.com, so they only consider impressions and clicks that occur on Google.com when calculating and applying quality score for keywords entered into Google.com auctions.

This also means that when looking at CTRs in AdWords reports, you have to be careful to not look at the blended Search + Display numbers, but at the CTR for Search instead. Even then, you'll see the influence of clicks on the Search Partners Network, which is not used in quality score calculations. Once again, there is no way to see the numbers that really matter.

The performance of your keywords and ads in all other available channels (which are collectively called the Google Network to distinguish them from Google.com) are used in distinct quality score calculations for each channel. In other words, your CTR on the Display Network impacts your results and costs on the Display Network, your CTR in mobile search impacts your results and costs in mobile search, and so on.

The point is, if you choose to run ads on any non-Google.com networks, it will not negatively affect your quality score for ads that run on Google.com search results.

> *CTR on the Google Network only ever impacts quality score on the Google Network—not on Google.com*
>
> Source: http://goo.gl/vG4A0

The Role of Visible CTR in Quality Score

Since click-through rate is the driving factor behind the calculation of quality score, it would be natural to think about it in terms of the CTR reported for each keyword in your account.

But as we've learned, this simple keyword-level CTR isn't used by AdWords to calculate quality score. Instead, four rather obscure versions of CTR are used, at least two of which are not reported anywhere. Things are further complicated by the fact that visible quality score is based on a different set of rules and data.

Google seems to be saying:

- ♦ Quality Score is critical to your success.

- ♦ Click-through rates are an important component in quality score.

- ♦ Four specific click-through rates drive quality score, but . . .

- ♦ You can't (easily) see any of these metrics.

Why can't you see these metrics? Because they're either not available at all or not available in a usable format:

- ♦ **The historical CTR of the keyword and the matched ad on Google**. Not available in the AdWords interface. You can create downloadable reports that include this data, but those CTRs blend the Google Network and the Search Partners Network.

- ♦ **The historical CTR of the account**. Available in AdWords as listed above, but with no indication of how much history is used or how any of it is weighted.

- ♦ **The historical CTR of the display URLs**. Not available in the AdWords interface, although you can export all text ad records and manually combine and weight the CTRs.

- ♦ **Performance in the geography where the ad is shown**. Not available in the AdWords interface. It is not possible to access this data.

You're supposed to optimize quality score, but in fact all you can optimize or really know very much about at all is visible quality score. There really isn't even any way to know how different the two are in any case because the outputs (except for the rather unimportant first page bid estimate) are just as hidden and unavailable as the inputs. There is no available reporting on eligibility, ad rank, or cpc at the keyword-query-ad copy level.

How Keyword CTR Correlates with Visible Quality Score

Given that the actual metrics aren't readily available in reports, how good of a proxy for these specialized CTRs is the plain old keyword-level CTR?

The answer appears to be "pretty good," at least in terms of how it relates to visible quality score.

In an October 2009 post on SearchEngineLand, Siddharth Shah of Efficient Frontier documented that Keyword CTR has a strong correlation to visible quality score. In the article, he shows how quality scores from 1 to 8 are clearly correlated to keyword click-through rate, and that keywords with quality scores of 9 or 10 are the result of a very large jump in CTR as compared to those with lower quality scores. Mr. Shah analyzed data from a number of different accounts, although only a single large advertiser (over 500,000 keywords in a single AdWords account) was used to produce the graph below.

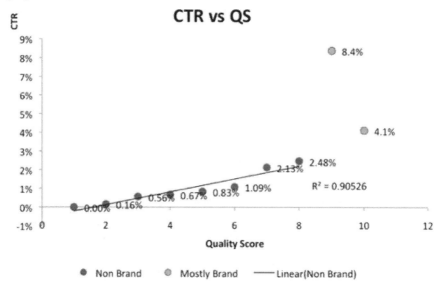

We have independently confirmed similar relationships in the accounts of many advertisers. So even though the actual calculations of quality score are based on more specific forms of CTR, and you should consider those forms when making management decisions, it *is* worthwhile to consider reported keyword CTR as representative of your progress and indicative of your quality score results.

Exceptions may exist, but generally speaking, higher average CTRs lead to higher visible quality scores.

One thing to note is that, as pointed out in the chart above, keywords that earn quality scores of 9 or 10 almost always display a significant jump in CTR over those that earn 7 or below. This is most likely explained by the observation that when keywords do better than average, they frequently do a lot better than average. This explains the spikes in the graph above and those that we've seen in our own analyses of a great many accounts. This is also consistent with the fact that most, but certainly not all, keywords that earn quality scores of 8, 9, or 10 are brand keywords enjoying stratospheric click-through rates.

Remember that despite these trends, there isn't a consistent test for a specific CTR to achieve a specific quality score. The CTR necessary to earn a 7 for one keyword or in one industry can be very different than the CTR required to earn a 7 for another keyword or in another industry. The answer to the question "What CTR is required to earn a quality score of 7?" is always "It depends."

Factor 2: Relevance

Relevance has always been close to Google's heart, so it's not surprising that it's prominently applied within the quality score calculation. The question is, even after all these years, what does relevance really mean?

Relevance is the mystery inside the secret of quality score. It often seems that Google defines relevance the way the Supreme Court once defined pornography: there is no precise definition, but Google knows it when they see it.

In fact, AdWords help provides this rather circular definition of relevance and quality:

> *Relevance refers to the usefulness of information to a user (such as an ad, keyword, or landing page). Relevance, or the quality of an ad, is reflected by a keyword's quality score. The AdWords system is designed to match our users' needs as closely as possible to relevant ads. This ensures a positive user experience so that users click on AdWords ads more often, while maintaining the advertising value the program provides to our advertisers.*

Source: http://goo.gl/3Gt68

In other words, relevance is reflected by a keyword's quality score—and quality score is a measure of relevance. Any questions?

Google has taken a simple and well-understood concept and made it confusing and frustrating. This has resulted in a lot of frustrated advertisers and paid search managers.

Let's try to demystify it a bit.

The Secret of Relevance

Everyone knows the dictionary definition of "relevance." And most advertisers and even PPC experts assume this meaning applies to the way Google uses the word in the context of quality score. But like the word "quality" itself, Google has a way of using common terms in somewhat puzzling ways.

If relevance meant what we all think it means, it wouldn't be possible to bid on the keyword "gold plated microphone," match it with ad copy that says "Best prices on gold plated microphones," send people to www.gold-plated-microphones.com to find a page full of gold plated microphone details, and still be told you have a relevance problem.

And the keyword "Sugar Free Coke" must clearly be relevant to a query for "Diet Soda" and perfectly relevant to a query for "Sugar Free Coke." Right?

Nope.

The problem is that Google isn't using the dictionary definition of "relevance" when they refer to it in terms of quality score. They aren't checking to see if words or concepts are identical or similar or related. Relevance is not determined by considering the consistency of words or meanings between search queries, keywords, ad copy, and landing pages. Not even using keywords in your ad copy or landing pages will directly affect relevance. That's just not the way AdWords measures it in this capacity. There is no semantic analysis involved.

Instead, Google uses an indirect measure of relevance: searcher behavior. They determine whether a keyword and text ad copy combination is relevant to a search query based primarily, if not entirely, on the feedback searchers provide them when they vote with their clicks.

That's right—our old friend CTR is the secret driver behind relevance.

Yes, really.

These facts were confirmed by Google during interviews conducted for this book. AdWords performs no semantic or linguistic analysis comparing your keywords to your ad copy or the text on your landing pages. Including keywords in ad copy does not inherently improve relevance or quality score, and including keywords on landing pages does not inherently improve landing page quality scores. The only things that improve relevance are things that get more clicks.

Of course, including keywords or related terms in ad copy, target URLs, and landing pages may very well incite users to click—but it's the results, rather than the existence or inclusion of words or their meanings, that are beneficial. To be successful, your choices just have to earn clicks. Words can be dictionary relevant, but if they don't get clicks, they're not relevant as far as AdWords is concerned. If ad copy that is funny but unrelated earns clicks, that's a great strategy and can earn excellent quality scores.

Why Google Says "Relevance" When They Mean CTR

In our discussions, we learned that the term "relevance" is refers to a distinct set of measures and tests—including query-specific measures and geo-specific measures—that, taken together, act as a type of filter for ad quality that is distinct from information gathered from the other CTR measures described earlier in this chapter. It seems that the CTR-related measures included in the "relevance" bucket are specific factors that Google is comfortable using as a kind of "quality score modifier," but that wouldn't work well or at all if considered in the broader ways of the other CTR measures. The exact reasons remain undisclosed, but this is how it works.

To get a slightly better appreciation for this distinction, look at how Google uses the word "relevance" in this note about the role of search queries:

> *The Quality Score used to determine ad position depends on the relevance of your keyword to the search query. This Quality Score is often higher if the search query matches the keyword exactly. However, this does not depend on whether your keyword's match type is broad, phrase, or exact. For example, the broad-match keyword "tennis shoes" would have the same Quality Score in relationship to the search query "tennis shoes" as it would if it were an exact match.*

Source: http://goo.gl/UBi91

Advertisers may wish Google had replaced the word "relevance" with "CTR" in the paragraph above. But by using relevance, they're signaling that not just any CTR will suffice. In this case, relevance means a set of specific and precise CTR measures, such as those equal to the current searcher's query, geography, time of day, and any number of other very specific factors that may influence CTR or help Google predict the performance of that keyword in those conditions.

It also makes sense that by using the word "relevance" and knowing the assumptions people make about what that word means, Google is promoting the kind of behavior and decision making that will in most cases drive good organization, ad copy, landing page selection, and CTR. Being relevant in the eye of the searcher is important and drives higher click-through rates, and tight contextual alignment is almost always the best way to get there.

By telling you that you have to be relevant instead of telling you to get high CTRs, Google is telling you not just what to do, but how to do it.

Reviewing Relevance Ratings

You can view the relevance rating for any keyword in AdWords by clicking the thought bubble in the Status column under the Keywords tab. The pop-up that appears lists keyword relevance as "Poor" or "No Problems."

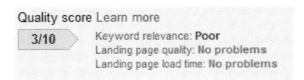

If the keyword is rated "No problem,'" then accept that your relevance is good and don't worry about it for that particular keyword.

If the keyword is rated "Poor," then you should urgently work either to improve the alignment of your ad copy with your keyword and the search queries it is attracting, or reconsider the appropriateness of the keyword to your current account. If you can't fix the relevance problem, you'll need to rewrite the copy, pause the keyword, or accept a low quality score and its ramifications.

Two Kinds of Relevance

Even though relevance is measured in terms of click-through rates, it's still worth thinking about how to make your keywords and ads more directly focused toward the searchers you want to reach because doing will drive you to take actions that may increase CTR or help you to understand why CTR or quality score is lower than you might have expected. In other words, dictionary relevance still matters, even if it's not being measured.

Google uses the word "relevance" twice on their list of quality score factors. The first mentions "the relevance of the keyword to the ads in its ad group," and the other calls out "the relevance of the keyword and the matched ad to the search query." These two factors sound similar, but we believe they're actually quite distinct, and this distinction is important.

Below we introduce vertical relevance and horizontal relevance, to describe the different ways that your keywords might relate to the population of search queries that they might be matched to in search results. Google isn't directly measuring these types of relevance as such, but we believe that these ideas will help you to structure your accounts effectively and make better decisions in expanding and targeting keywords in your account.

Vertical Relevance

The idea expressed by "the relevance of the keyword to the ads in its ad group" is something we'll call *vertical relevance*. It concerns how closely the keyword matches or aligns to the other elements of the search, such as the query and the ad copy. It's about whether or not your advertising is tightly focused on one clear and specific topic or idea.

For example, the keyword "organic dog food" would be highly relevant to a search query of "natural dog food," especially if the text ad copy mentioned "healthy organic dry dog food." On the other hand, the keyword "puppy care" wouldn't be very relevant to a query for "organic dog food" because feeding is only one of the many aspects of puppy care.

Vertical relevance is controlled by adding only keywords to your ad groups only if they are clearly related to the text ad copy (and landing pages) and the product or service you're marketing. It can be improved by writing ads (and landing pages) that align very precisely with the ad groups' keywords.

Vertical relevance is often challenged when keywords are "expanded" to include words and phrases that refer to related topics not directly related to your offering. If you sell swimming pool products and start adding keywords about summer, for example, vertical relevance starts to decline because the keywords are about a season and the ad copy is about pool products.

Horizontal Relevance

The idea of "the relevance of the keyword and the matched ad to the search query" considers something we'll call *horizontal relevance*: the degree to which your advertising (the keyword and ad copy) addresses the intent of people who search on matching queries. It's about how broadly your ad copy's text covers the range of possible meanings of the search queries it attracts.

Suppose you bid on the keyword "glory days" because that's the name of your best-selling line of summer clothing. But if some of the people who search with the query "glory days" are looking for a gospel record, and some of them are looking for the lyrics to a Bruce Springsteen song, and only some of them are looking for your apparel, your keyword has poor horizontal relevance. In other words, your ad is not what many of those searchers are looking for, no matter how great your ad copy, and as a result your click-through rates will suffer.

You can't really control the horizontal relevance of a keyword. Some words and phrases are associated with a wide range of meanings or intents. No matter how you organize your ad groups or write your text ad copy for such keywords, through no fault of your own some (or many) searchers will not think your ad is relevant to them. Ads displayed in results for this type of keyword are almost certain to earn very low click-through rates, which yield very low quality scores.

If ten different people might use the same single word to mean ten different specific things, the horizontal relevance for that word will be low no matter which of the ten you intended when you bid on that keyword. Consider the word "comfortable," as an admittedly extreme example—it could refer to shoes or beds or air temperature or a thousand other things. If you offer the world's most comfortable headphones, most people who type the world "comfortable" into Google aren't looking for you, even if that's your branding and positioning, even if it's in your product name. The horizontal relevance of that keyword will be poor, and the CTR low, for any advertiser who tries to use it.

The only way to avoid horizontal relevance problems is to choose and use specific and focused keywords that will likely be matched to specific or focused search queries. Adding more words to a phrase generally increases the horizontal relevance, as does using domain-specific terminology. Anything that increases the precision or narrows the meaning of your keywords increases the chance for high CTRs and therefore high quality scores.

Of course, when you limit your keyword list to very specific and focused words and phrases, you reduce the size of the audience you can target. This is the tradeoff for achieving good relevance that Google implies but never states outright. Perhaps they're afraid to come right out and say that trying to advertise on non-specific keywords is not a good idea because it will result in low CTRs and quality scores.

Search Results without Paid Ads

Horizontal relevance (and its impact on CTR and therefore quality score) also explains another mysterious AdWords phenomenon: search results that include few or no paid ads even though many advertisers are trying (or have tried) to advertise on those keywords.

Search results frequently include very few or zero paid ads when the search query is a very general term. A search for "Philadelphia," for example, returns only a single paid ad (for a tour-guide company), while a search for "Philadelphia hotel" yields eight different ads.

This happens not because there aren't a lot of advertisers bidding on the keyword "Philadelphia," butbecause people searching for "Philadelphia" might be looking for many different things: hotels, dining, sports teams, local businesses, or something else entirely. Very few ads that have been run against this keyword have proven relevant to more than a small percentage of the searchers. No individual advertiser (except tour guides, apparently)

seems able to attract a high enough overall percentage of the clicks to justify a good quality score. And Google decided they'd rather show few or no ads than ads that are irrelevant to most searchers.

If you bid on a keyword like this, you're likely to get a poor keyword relevance rating due to this horizontal relevance problem.

> *In order to be consistent with our philosophy of showing the right ad to the right user at the right time, we'd rather show no ads on a page than show low-quality ads. That's why you might find that there are no ads on a page, even when an advertiser is bidding on the query that generated those results.*

Source: http://goo.gl/rY1sp

FINAL THOUGHTS ON RELEVANCE

Relevance helps everybody, and Google clearly strives for it. Understanding that both vertical relevance (alignment with and for the individual searcher) and horizontal relevance (alignment with the broad search population) can play a role adds a new perspective to managing the elements of your account that drive quality score. Knowing that it's technically based on CTR and not content analysis puts the pressure on performance and results.

There was something natural and fitting about Google measuring "dictionary relevance," so it's a little unsettling to find out they don't actually do it. It turns out that relevance is whatever works.

This view of relevance serves Google, searchers, and ultimately advertisers well. It penalizes and discourages advertisers from trying to advertise beyond the range of a tightly focused target market. And it shows yet again that Google only wants people to advertise where they'll be successful.

Factor 3: Landing Page Quality

Landing page quality is perhaps the least clear and most broadly misunderstood component of quality score. In various writings, Google delivers mixed signals about the importance and impact of landing pages; they seem to want to suggest landing pages play a large role but the details tend to suggest something a little bit less.

> *The quality of a landing page is represented by such things as the usefulness and relevance of information provided on the page, ease of navigation for the user, page loading times, how many links are on the page, how links are used on the page, and more.*

Source: http://goo.gl/PZlpt

Conventional wisdom says that landing pages play a key role in what we're calling vertical relevance—they're supposed to reflect the same narrow subject and (if possible) terminology as the keyword, text ad, and search query in order to help drive a high relevance rating.

Google reinforces this idea in their Landing Page and Site Quality Guidelines when talking about landing page:

> *Users should easily be able to find what your ad promises. Link to the page on your site that provides the most useful information about the product or service in your ad. For instance, direct users to the page where they can buy the advertised product, rather than to a page with a description of several products.*
>
> *We've found that when our advertisers' sites reflect these guidelines, two important things happen:*
>
> *The money that you spend on AdWords ads will be more likely to turn into paying customers.*
>
> *Users develop a trust in the positive experience that is provided after clicking AdWords ads (and this turns into additional targeted leads for you).*
>
> Source: http://goo.gl/x9TOV

But while this kind of tight conceptual alignment may have the described benefits to your business and results, it is not considered in the calculation of quality score. The official description of factors that influence quality score (as listed earlier in this chapter) refers rather cryptically to "the quality of your landing page," but Google has confirmed that landing page quality score is not improved by the presence or absence of any specific copy. Instead, landing page quality score is almost entirely a measure of whether or not a page delivers a poor experience to the searcher.

Google's Landing Page and Site Quality Guidelines (http://goo.gl/EH1eL) provide an extensive list of the things your landing pages and overall website should do to avoid account bans or poor landing page quality scores.

The list is divided into three sections—Relevant and Original Content, Transparency, and Navigability—and includes all kinds of common sense best practices that legitimate businesses would want to (and probably already) follow.

There are many specific characteristics of landing pages that Google wants to discourage or prevent: irrelevant content, slow landing page load time, missing links to privacy policy, tricky redirects, involuntary software installs, and other negative attributes:

Data collection sites that offer free items, etc. in order to collect private information.

Arbitrage sites that are designed for the purpose of displaying ads.

Low quality affiliate sites, such as poor comparison shopping or aggregation sites whose primary purpose is to send users to other comparison sites rather than to provide useful content or additional search functionality.

"Get-rich quick" sites.

Sites that go against Google's Software Principles, such as malware sites that install software on a visitor's computer.

Sites that feature false or misleading claims or misappropriated content (including competitive claims, generic superlatives, unauthorized use of trademarks or copyrighted content, false endorsements, scams and other types of false or deceptive claims and content).

Sites that go against Google's Webmaster Guidelines, such as those that use cloaking or other inappropriate technologies.

Source: http://goo.gl/WwSxS

What Google is saying is: "Play fair. Be nice." They're making it clear that when they see any of these negative behaviors, they will block keywords entirely or assign a low quality score that drives the cost of pointing to such a landing page up.

And in case that isn't clear enough, Google reiterates elsewhere that some landing page– or business model–related penalties may be permanent. Google has frequently banned advertisers "for life" for serious landing page quality score violations.

> *When a site fails to follow our landing page and site policy guidelines, it may result in any of the following actions, depending on the severity:*
>
> * *disapproval of ads*
> * *account suspension*
> * *disabling of all ad traffic to your domain*
> * *automated suspension upon set-up of new accounts (ban from Google AdWords)*
>
> *Note: Pausing or deleting an ad or ad group won't remove the violation. The only way to remove the violation is by fixing the related site based on our landing page and site policy guidelines.*
>
> Source: http://goo.gl/n4hyx

You need to take the rules and these warnings seriously.

REVIEWING LANDING PAGE AND SITE QUALITY

There are two kinds of problems related to landing pages and your web site in general. The first are policy violations – elements of your pages or site that Google considers potentially unsafe, unscrupulous, or illegal. When they detect policy violations, your site is suspended and your account is effectively shut down.

When this occurs, you will see "Site suspended" in the Status column of the Keywords tab in AdWords. All keywords in the entire account will be suspended for any site policy infraction.

	Keyword	Ad group	Status	Max. CPC	Clicks
☐ ●	t-shirts	Shirts	💬 Site suspended ?	$1.00	
☐ ●	buy shirts	Shirts	💬 Site suspended ?	$1.00	
☐ ●	t-shirts online	Shirts	💬 Site suspended ?	$1.00	
☐ ●	cool t-shirts	Shirts	💬 Site suspended ?	$1.00	
	Total - Search ?				
	Total - Display Network ?				
	Total - all keywords				

Ad groups   Settings   Ads   Keywords   Networks

All but deleted keywords ▼   Segment ▼   Filter ▼   Columns ▼

➕ Add keywords   Edit ▼   Change status... ▼   See search terms... ▼   Alerts ▼   Autom

The second are factors that would lower the quality of the user experience for people who visit your landing pages or site. These include issues like page load time, use of original content, or availability of a privacy policy. These types of problems can result in a "Poor" landing page quality, reduce your quality score for CPC, and increase first page bid estimates.

Quality score Learn more

5/10	Keyword relevance: No problems Landing page quality: No problems Landing page load time: No problems

You can get an indication of how AdWords rates your landing page quality (they've taken to calling it a "grade") by clicking on the thought bubble in the Status column under the Keyword tab in AdWords. The pop-up that appears lists both the landing page quality and landing page load time status.

> *Each of your keywords will receive a landing page quality grade that can be viewed by using keyword diagnosis. The grade is based on the average quality of the landing pages in the ad group and of any landing pages in the rest of the account with the same domain. If multiple ad groups have landing pages with the same domain, therefore, the keywords in all these ad groups will have identical landing page quality grades.*
>
> Source: http://goo.gl/ObKFc

The good news is that if these say "No Problems," then they mean it. Unless you get a "Poor" landing page score, your landing pages have effectively nothing to do with your quality scores.

> *If keyword diagnosis shows that your landing page quality is graded "No problems," your Quality Score will not be affected. If your landing page quality is graded "Poor," your Quality Score will be negatively affected.*
>
> Source: http://goo.gl/ObKFc

So now we know that landing pages can't help quality scores; they can only hurt. But when they hurt, they can hurt badly. AdWords recently added another indication that there are problems with your landing page or website; when they find policy violations on your landing page or website, the Status column in the Keywords tab will say "Site suspended." When this happens, no quality score will be calculated for the impacted keywords and they will get zero impressions.

> *The primary purpose of landing page policy is to make sure that the sites to which users are taken after clicking on ads are safe, trustworthy, and legal. Automated systems and trained specialists make policy enforcement decisions. When landing pages are suspected of violating AdWords policies, ads and keywords linked to them are disabled and not allowed to enter the AdWords auction.*

Source: http://goo.gl/MYrvh

The only resolution for a suspended site is to correct the offending issues and appeal to Google for reinstatement. See *Chapter Ten: Dealing with Disaster* for more information.

THE IMPACT OF LANDING PAGES ON QUALITY SCORE

Landing pages play an interesting and somewhat confusing role in quality score due to the fact that their impact is limited to certain versions of quality score.

♦ **Poor landing page quality does impact visible quality score**. And in most cases it has a significant effect. When keywords are showing visible quality scores below 6, it's a good idea to check to see if "Poor" landing page quality score is the reason.

♦ **Landing pages are excluded from the calculation of ad rank**. When determining the order in which ads will appear, AdWords uses quality score for ad rank, which is calculated without considering landing pages. This means that you can earn the #1 spot (or any other good position) even if you have a very bad landing page.

> *For calculating a keyword-targeted ad's position, landing page quality is not a factor.*

Source: http://goo.gl/l98iK

♦ **Landing page quality score is used in the calculation of cost per click**. Once you've earned your position, you have to pay for it. And if you have a low landing page quality score, you're going to pay a lot more because the landing page quality score is included in quality score for CPC.

> *As a component of your keywords' overall Quality Scores, a high landing page quality score can . . . decrease your keywords' cost per clicks (CPCs).*

> Source: http://goo.gl/4caBK

♦ **Landing page quality score is used in the calculation of the first page bid estimate**. Since the first page bid estimate (FPBE) is a prediction of the bid necessary to get a position on page one with your current quality score, it makes sense that the impact of your landing page is included in this calculation.

So a "Poor" landing page score will lower your visible quality score, not impact your ability to get into auctions or earn good positions, and dramatically increase the CPCs you pay when those ads are clicked.

How Often Are Landing Pages Reviewed?

Unlike just about every other element of the AdWords system (and Google in general), landing pages are not reviewed in real time, or even quickly or frequently. Generally, it appears that landing pages are reviewed within a few days of when first used as target URLs within AdWords. But after that, if the page changes and the target URLs don't, it can be days, weeks, or even months before the page is reevaluated.

> *If you've made significant changes to improve the relevance and quality of your landing pages, you should see higher Quality Scores for your keywords. You probably won't see an impact within the first few days, but should see results over the next several months.*

> Source: http://goo.gl/sXb9W

This can be frustrating when waiting for AdWords to notice improvements to your landing pages. To force AdWords to look at your page quickly after you've made improvements, consider using a new target URL. This gets the page prioritized as a new crawl rather than a regular review.

When the crawler does finally review any landing page, the results supersede all previous visits:

> *Google does not keep track of your landing page quality history. While there may be some delay between times when Google crawls your landing page, we only use the latest crawl of your page to determine your Quality Score.*

Source: http://goo.gl/e3iyp

Some advertisers have used the slow (or, some believe, non-existent) landing page reevaluation to their benefit, putting up one initial landing page for Google to review and then swapping it for another once they believe Google has set the landing page quality score and is unlikely (in the advertiser's opinion or experience) to reevaluate it. It's a risky tactic, but one that some more adventurous advertisers have used to their perceived advantage.

LAST THOUGHTS ON LANDING PAGE QUALITY

AdWords uses the landing page quality measure to punish what it sees as bad or questionable advertisers. A "Poor" landing page quality score acts like a barrier to prevent eligibility into many auctions and a tax imposed on your cost per click. If your landing pages are outside the guidelines, or are thought to be, it can hurt badly. This is a clear and important fact of life; it's difficult to be successful with landing page quality problems.

While site policy violations may result in a temmporary suspension of all of your keywords, in most cases landing page quality problems result only in fewer impressions and higher CPCs. You won't be prevented from advertising (because the landing page score isn't factored into the calculation of ad rank). So you can at least partially spend your way out of the problem.

Clearly Google is walking a fine line here, balancing user experience with an advertiser's right to advertise despite not following the guidelines. If problems are too bad, the advertiser (or their ads) is banned. But if the problems are minor, the ads run with a penalty of lower quality scores and higher prices—a penalty the advertiser will hopefully notice and correct.

Landing pages are an important part of the experience users have with your site, and they contribute greatly to a user's post-click behavior. There are many reasons to work to improve landing pages, but if they're not getting "Poor" quality score rankings, then quality score is not one of those reasons.

Weighting the Quality Score Factors

Given the number of elements that influence quality score, it's natural to ask how big a role each plays in the actual calculation.

When Google's chief economist, Dr. Hal Varian, answered that question, he said click-through rates represent about 60% of the quality score calculation, relevance represents about 25%, and "other factors" fill out the remaining 15% or so of the pie. But Google doesn't generally talk in such specific terms, and this information isn't found in the AdWords help system.

In reality, any effort to define these allocations is only useful for giving new and less experienced advertisers or search managers a simple mental model of the influential factors. It's a way to shape perceptions and influence behavior. The percentages mentioned above are not, technically or literally, the way the elements are weighted, but are rather more of an average or theoretical idea.

There are two reasons why the "How much weight does each factor have?" question cannot be answered:

1. The factors aren't nearly as simple and limited as the stock descriptions suggest. As explained throughout this chapter, none of the components are as simple as they first appear, and each of them have many sub-elements that may or may not apply or be available at any given time.

2. The evolving nature of Google's effort—the goal of making the best prediction of future behavior based on the most and best available information possible—requires that the weight of the components constantly evolve as more data becomes available and the quality of different pieces of data improves.

When an account is new, the available history of the selected keywords as used by other advertisers may be the only information available in any substantial volume. When new keywords are added to an account that has a substantial history, the CTR history of the account or the display URLs may be the best clue as to future performance for those keywords.

As time passes and impression counts grow, the amount of specific data on all the variations of CTR expands. When there is a lot of history for a keyword and its assigned ad copy, as well as the keyword against many common search queries and for searches from many popular geographies, it makes sense that the influence of more distant signals would be reduced considerably.

Penalties, as labeled in this book, are the great exception. When Google finds or thinks you're behaving badly, they'll make it impossible to earn good quality scores no matter how you configure or manage your account. These include the kinds of landing page issues discussed earlier in this chapter or the business model or target market penalties that will be covered in *Chapter Nine: Quality Score Management Basics*.

Chapter Summary

According to Google's official description, three primary components drive quality score: click-through rate, relevance, and landing pages. There is also some minor influence from an undisclosed set of "other factors." But the devil is in the detail of how those terms are defined and applied:

♦   The click-through rate they're talking about isn't the metric reported in your AdWords interface.

♦   Relevance isn't used the way any dictionary in the world defines it.

♦   Landing pages are only considered when they're poor.

In practical terms, quality score is all about click-through rate unless you're doing something wrong enough to get penalized. But to make that information actionable, you need to know the specific CTR versions that matter (account history, keyword + ad, and display URL), plus understand the potential impact of geography. Play those right, and higher CTRs will produce better quality scores in a very reliable manner.

This makes sense. A quality keyword and a quality ad are the ones that users click on. The higher the CTR of a keyword, the better it serves all three parties that Google is trying to please and optimize: Clicks mean site visitors to you. Clicks mean dollars to Google. And clicks mean that searchers are finding results that appeal to them.

Here's how most advertisers and paid search managers should think about the factors that drive quality score:

- **Click-through rates** are the key. Consider the way keywords are matched with specific text ads, prune underperforming ad copy ruthlessly, watch how specific display URLs perform, and remember that every keyword in the account impacts the overall account CTR history.

- **Relevance** matters, but not because Google is measuring it. Tightly aligned keywords, ad copy, and landing pages tend to increase some specific forms of click-through rates that Google considers indications of relevance. But if a keyword means too many different things to too many different people, it can be difficult or impossible to produce a CTR that will earn a good quality score no matter how contextually aligned your campaign components are.

- **Landing pages** are either a critical factor or a non-factor. Your pages must deliver reasonable performance and a good user experience, and avoid anything Google considers "funny business." If you meet these criteria, your keywords will see the quality scores their CTRs earn. Mess up on any of it, and a big wet blanket will be placed over the quality scores of some or all of the keywords in your account; earning anything other than very poor quality scores will be difficult or impossible.

Now See the Movie

Google has released a YouTube video that does a great job of introducing the factors that impact quality score and how they're weighted in the calculation.

In this video, Google Chief Economist Dr. Hal Varian discusses how AdWords works and many of the basic concepts of quality score. He talks about how the system impacts and interacts with advertisers, searchers, and AdWords itself. The video is an overview, and doesn't cover many of the advanced topics and issues, but it's definitely worth watching at http://goo.gl/Rtr3s.

Chapter Six:
The Impact of Quality Score

Quality score improves or degrades the performance of every keyword in your account every time a related search is conducted. It determines the success of your account in terms of both reach and profitability. In this chapter, we'll look at all the ways, large and small, that quality score impacts your AdWords account.

The AdWords system is pretty clear about how quality score is applied throughout the auction process:

> *Quality score is used in several different ways, including influencing your keywords' actual cost per clicks (CPCs) and estimating the first page bids that you see in your account. It also partly determines if a keyword is eligible to enter the ad auction that occurs when a user enters a search query and, if it is, how high the ad will be ranked.*

Source: http://goo.gl/oyG36

> *If your quality score is low, you may be using keywords, ads, or landing pages that aren't as targeted or relevant as they could be. This can mean higher cost-per-clicks and a potentially poor return on your investment.*

Source: http://goo.gl/1IUjQ

These quotes make clear that there are four decisions Google makes about each of your keywords based on quality score:

1. **Eligibility**. Every time someone executes a search, Google runs an auction to determine which ads will appear on the search results page. Before the auction starts, they determine which keywords/ads are eligible and appropriate to enter the auction (in other words, which keywords/ads have a chance to be displayed in the search results). The quality score of your keyword helps decide whether or not it is eligible to be in the ad auction.

2. **Rank/Position**. Once your keyword has entered the auction, quality score is a major factor in whether or not your ad earns one of the available slots, and if so, which position your ad takes on the search results page.

3. **Cost Per Click**. After the auction is complete, Google then determines the price each ad will cost if clicked. The keyword quality score is the key driver for how much you're charged for each click.

4. **First Page Bid Estimate**. Once a keyword has a quality score, Google assigns a first page bid estimate to keywords that would often not get ranked on the first page of search results for the search queries they match. The lower the quality score, the higher the first page bid estimate.

This makes it clear why it's so important to maximize your quality score: it's used in the calculations that determine when and where your ads are run and how much you have to pay for the clicks they generate. In this chapter, we'll review each of these impacts in greater detail.

Quality Score Impact One:

Eligibility

When someone types in a search query and clicks "Search" on Google, a lot of things happen in a very short period of time. The most important (for our purposes) is that Google decides which potential advertisers have keywords and ads that could be shown as part of the search results.

First, they compare the search query with the keywords and match type combinations that advertisers have purchased. The exact-match and phrase-match keyword decisions are fairly straightforward, while the broad-match decisions are more complex. Those are determined by Google's ad-matching algorithm, which looks at your keywords and their meanings, the search query, and the match type to decide if the keyword is relevant enough to a particular query to consider showing the ad.

Next, Google confirms that budget is available for the campaign to run ads. No budget, no entry into the auction.

Here's what Google says happens next:

> *The AdWords system evaluates your keyword for each auction and calculates its quality score. The quality score is based on the recent performance of the keyword and your ad, how relevant the two are to the search query, and other relevance factors.*

> *The AdWords system then calculates a cost-per-click (CPC) bid requirement based on this quality score, which applies only for this auction. The higher the score, the lower the bid requirement, and vice versa. If the keyword's CPC bid doesn't meet the requirement, the keyword can't trigger an ad for this particular auction.*

> Source: http://goo.gl/uhpXi

BID REQUIREMENTS AND MISSED AUCTIONS

The quote above is the perhaps the only time Google ever mentions "bid requirement," a variable that isn't often discussed in paid search circles either. Quality score helps to define the bid requirement, and your bid either hits or misses the bid requirement for eligibility in a particular auction. This means that every time a keyword's quality score declines, the bid requirement in related auctions increases, and the keyword loses eligibility for additional auctions.

In effect, the bid requirement sets a minimum ad rank (ad rank = bid x quality score) for eligibility into any auction. Once Google knows your quality score, they know whether or not your bid is high enough. When search results have only one or two visible paid ads, often there were other advertisers bidding on related keywords, but their bids didn't meet the bid requirement given their current quality score.

> *It's worth noting that every keyword has a minimum bid that is unique to how successfully that word has been used in an advertiser's particular account. So the minimum bid for the keyword "Kansas City BBQ sauce" will be different in your account than in your next door neighbor's account, who happens to be using the same keyword.*

Source: http://goo.gl/Mf6ij

The actual bid requirement is not disclosed even after it's been calculated. Google instead recommends that you look at the first page bid estimate, which seems to functions as an average bid requirement for a keyword across the various search queries and conditions in which it is used. When your max CPC is lower than the first page bid estimate for any keyword, you can expect that the keyword is missing out on some auctions for which it could be eligible.

Tracking Missed Eligibility with Impression Share

There is no way to know how often your keywords are not shown in auctions for which they could have been eligible. It would be great if there were a metric (perhaps called "potential") that could be compared to the "impressions" metric in order to understand this ratio. You can see, however, how often keywords were eligible for auctions but whose ads were ultimately not displayed via the impression share metrics. Unfortunately, these are campaign-level numbers so they don't tell you anything about the performance of individual keywords.

If your impression share or impression share exact values are low for any campaigns, you'll usually find that most of the loss is due to ad rank. This of course means that either raising the bid or the quality score would result in increased eligibility and impressions.

You can view your impression share by adding the Impression Share, Lost IS (budget), and Lost IS (rank) columns to campaign reports in AdWords via the Edit Columns menu.

☑ **Competitive metrics**
☑ Impr. share
☑ Lost IS (budget)
☑ Lost IS (rank)

To see Impression Share Exact Match, you must build a custom segment as described at http://goo.gl/57gCL, or you can build a report in the Dimensions tab by customizing the columns to include "campaign" and what they call "competitive metrics." This tells you how often your ads were not shown when the search query was identical to your keywords—a generally inexcusable omission.

Quality Score Impact Two:

Ad Position

Once it's been decided which keywords and advertisers are eligible to enter an auction, Google goes about the business of ranking and rating the candidates to determine the order in which their ads may be shown in the search results. Quality score plays a key role in this decision.

According to Google:

> *Ads are positioned on search and content pages based on their Ad Rank. The ad with the highest Ad Rank appears in the first position, and so on down the page.*

Source: http://goo.gl/mwb1R

Ad rank is calculated using the following formula:

Ad Rank = CPC bid (Max CPC) × quality score

This makes it clear that bids alone do not determine how highly your ads appear on a search results page. Bids and quality score contribute equally to ad rank, which means they play equal parts in determining the position in which your ads appear. You can improve the position of your ads by increasing your bid or by earning a higher quality score.

Keyword	Bid	QS	Ad Rank
Dylan Tickets	$ 3.00	1	3.00
Dylan Tix	$ 2.75	2	5.50
Tickets for Dylan	$ 2.50	3	7.50
Front row Dylan	$ 2.25	4	9.00
Dylan at Red Rocks	$ 2.00	5	10.00
Bob Dylan Tix	$ 1.75	6	10.50
Tickets Dylan Cheap	$ 1.50	7	10.50
Dylan Lawn Tickets	$ 1.25	8	10.00
Free Dylan Tickets	$ 1.00	9	9.00
Bob Dylan Seats	$ 0.75	10	7.50

The table above demonstrates this relationship by showing how bids and quality scores interact to produce ad ranks. A high bid with a low quality score produces a relatively low ad rank, while a low bid with a high quality scores earn a relative high ad rank. It takes two to tango. In this example, the advertiser with the highest bid ($3.00) earns the lowest ad rank, while a bidder in the middle of the pack ($1.50) ties for the highest ad rank (and therefore position) in the auction.

Since bids and quality scores contribute equally to the determination of ad position, both should get equal attention and resources in your management process. In fact, since quality score improvements last for some (potentially long) period of time, any investment in improving quality score would be a much better investment of resources. Think of quality score as "sweat equity"—an asset you earn with hard work instead of your credit card.

JUMPING TO A TOP POSITION

While the calculation of ad rank and the subsequent sorting of advertisers is the default way that ad position is determined, there is at least one override to these results. Depending on the keyword, and the bid and quality score of each advertiser, the order in which ads appear can change with selected ads jumping to higher positions on the top (rather the right edge) of the search results page.

Here's how Google explains it:

> *Up to three AdWords ads are eligible to appear above the search results (as opposed to on the side). Only ads that exceed a certain Quality Score and CPC bid threshold may appear in these positions. If the three highest-ranked ads all surpass these thresholds, then they'll appear in order above the search results. If one or more of these ads don't meet the thresholds, then the next highest-ranked ad that does will be allowed to show above the search results.*

> *The CPC bid threshold is determined by the matched keyword's Quality Score; the higher Quality Score, the lower the CPC threshold. This ensures that quality plays an even more important role in determining the ads that show above search results.*

Source: http://goo.gl/eTXV5

To understand the "jump on top" override, consider this example:

♦ **Keyword A**: quality score = 6, bid = $1.50, ad rank = 9.0
♦ **Keyword B**: quality score = 6, bid = $1.30, ad rank = 7.8
♦ **Keyword C**: quality score = 9, bid = $0.80, ad rank = 7.2

Based on their ad ranks, you'd expect keyword A to get the top slot, followed by keywords B and C. But in some cases, Google will promote keyword C above keywords A and B and place it on top, above the search results. This is a huge bonus, in this case earned for a quality score of 9 when competitive advertisers had all earned scores below 7.

There is apparently no way to determine which keywords are eligible to "jump on top," nor is there any way to know when it has happened (other than the impact on average position) to keywords in your account.

So quality score can ensure that a keyword is eligible for an auction, and it directly impacts which position the ad is assigned in the auction itself. If things are going well, your keyword made it in the door and earned you a good seat. In a moment, you'll find out how much the ticket costs.

Quality Score Impact Three:

The Price You Pay

After the auction is over and each keyword has been assigned a position based on its ad rank, the final step is for Google to use quality score to determine how they'll charge you if an ad is clicked.

Here how they describe the CPC calculation:

> *You always pay the lowest amount possible for the highest position you can get given your quality score and CPC bid.*
>
> *To find this amount, we divide the Ad Rank of the ad showing beneath you by your quality score, then round up to the nearest cent (we show this part of the formula as "+ $0.01" to keep things simple).*
>
> *Actual CPC = (Ad Rank to beat ÷ quality score) + $0.01*
>
> Source: http://goo.gl/e4YEF

Let's look at an example of all of these steps and the results.

1. We begin with a set of keywords with their bids, quality scores, and resulting ad ranks.

Pos	Keyword	Bid	QS	Ad Rank
1	Tickets Dylan Cheap	$ 1.50	7	10.50
2	Bob Dylan Tix	$ 1.75	6	10.50
3	Dylan Lawn Tickets	$ 1.25	8	10.00
4	Dylan at Red Rocks	$ 2.00	5	10.00
5	Free Dylan Tickets	$ 1.00	9	9.00
6	Front row Dylan	$ 2.25	4	9.00
7	Bob Dylan Seats	$ 0.75	10	7.50
8	Tickets for Dylan	$ 2.50	3	7.50
9	Dylan Tix	$ 2.75	2	5.50
10	Dylan Tickets	$ 3.00	1	3.00

2. Next, we sort these keywords from highest to lowest by ad rank to define the position each ad earns.

Keyword	Bid	QS	Ad Rank
Dylan Tickets	$ 3.00	1	3.00
Dylan Tix	$ 2.75	2	5.50
Tickets for Dylan	$ 2.50	3	7.50
Front row Dylan	$ 2.25	4	9.00
Dylan at Red Rocks	$ 2.00	5	10.00
Bob Dylan Tix	$ 1.75	6	10.50
Tickets Dylan Cheap	$ 1.50	7	10.50
Dylan Lawn Tickets	$ 1.25	8	10.00
Free Dylan Tickets	$ 1.00	9	9.00
Bob Dylan Seats	$ 0.75	10	7.50

3. Finally, the cost per click is calculated for each keyword by taking the ad rank from the keyword in the position beneath it, dividing that number by the keyword's own quality score, and adding $0.01. The lowest keyword pays the bid minimum that AdWords established for that keyword for this auction.

Pos	Keyword	Bid	QS	Ad Rank	CPC
1	Tickets Dylan Cheap	$ 1.50	7	10.50	$ 1.51
2	Bob Dylan Tix	$ 1.75	6	10.50	$ 1.68
3	Dylan Lawn Tickets	$ 1.25	8	10.00	$ 1.26
4	Dylan at Red Rocks	$ 2.00	5	10.00	$ 1.81
5	Free Dylan Tickets	$ 1.00	9	9.00	$ 1.01
6	Front row Dylan	$ 2.25	4	9.00	$ 1.89
7	Bob Dylan Seats	$ 0.75	10	7.50	$ 0.76
8	Tickets for Dylan	$ 2.50	3	7.50	$ 1.84
9	Dylan Tix	$ 2.75	2	5.50	$ 1.51
10	Dylan Tickets	$ 3.00	1	3.00	$ 0.85

As this demonstrates, keywords with low quality scores generally earn very poor positions and often much higher CPCs than adjacent keywords. This example also produces some other interesting results:

♦   The #1 position is earned by the seventh highest bidder.

♦   Four advertisers pay a CPC higher than the ad in position #1 even though they're in positions 2, 4, 6, and 8.

♦   The keyword with the highest quality score happened to have the lowest bid, and so it earned the seventh position.

♦   The keyword with the highest bid had the lowest quality score and is in the tenth position.

To be fair, this example has a fairly extreme inversion of bids and quality scores—higher bidders have low quality scores and low bidders have high quality scores—but it does highlight how these two values work together to establish position.

Pos	Keyword	Bid	QS	Ad Rank	CPC
7	Bob Dylan Seats	$ 1.25	10	12.50	$ 1.23
6	Front row Dylan	$ 3.05	4	12.20	$ 3.01
8	Tickets for Dylan	$ 4.00	3	12.00	$ 3.68
9	Dylan Tix	$ 5.50	2	11.00	$ 5.39
10	Dylan Tickets	$ 10.75	1	10.75	$ 10.51
1	Tickets Dylan Cheap	$ 1.50	7	10.50	$ 1.51
2	Bob Dylan Tix	$ 1.75	6	10.50	$ 1.68
3	Dylan Lawn Tickets	$ 1.25	8	10.00	$ 1.26
4	Dylan at Red Rocks	$ 2.00	5	10.00	$ 1.81
5	Free Dylan Tickets	$ 1.00	9	9.00	$ 0.85

Given the values in this example, bids would have to be increased dramatically for the keywords with the lowest quality scores to move into the top half of the results (as shown in the table below). Keywords with quality scores of 1 to 4 require bids anywhere from two to eight times higher than a keyword with quality score of 7, just to earn a top 5 position.

This demonstrates how powerful quality score is at driving both position and CPC. Any increase in quality score drives position higher and CPC lower. Any decrease in quality score moves position down and pushes CPC up.

It's also interesting to compare the role of quality score and bids (max CPC) in these calculations. Quality score impacts position with the same weight as bids, but it has a much more direct and substantial role on the calculation of CPC than bids does. The bid on a keyword isn't even used as part of the cost-per-click calculation; its only role is to contribute to the ad rank calculation that determines which competitor's ad rank is divided by your keyword's quality score to determine the CPC. Bids play a far less significant role in paid search than most people realize.

Without successful quality score management, it will be hard and expensive to earn as many impressions or as high a position as possible, and CPCs will be much higher for any clicks you do receive.

How Much Does Quality Score Save or Cost

Knowing the formula used to calculate cost per click, it would appear that you could calculate the impact of any specific quality score on CPC. The ad rank of the next highest advertiser is divided by your keyword's quality score, and then $0.01 is added to determine CPC. Mathematically, it's easy to calculate how much any number moves up or down when divided by a known range of numbers—such as 1 to 10.

So if the quality scores used to calculate CPC were really integers between 1 and 10, you could calculate the economic impact that any visible quality score would have on the CPC of that keyword. In that case, earning a quality score of 10 would provide a 30% discount on CPC as compared to a "neutral" quality score of 7, while a quality score of 5 would result in a 40% increase in CPC as compared to a quality score of 7. Knowing these impacts provides some context for the value and importance of improving quality score.

In the famous "Economics of Quality Score" post on the ClickEquations blog, this exact logic and math was used to produce the table shown below, which reports the relative cost impact of any quality score on any keyword.

But there is one serious problem with these calculations: quality score for CPC is very different than visible quality score. The distinctions between these versions of quality score were described in *Chapter Four: Which Quality Score*. They are each based on different components and, most importantly, they're not

Impact of Quality Score on CPC

If QS is:	Your CPC vs QS=7 is:	
10	Discounted by:	30.00%
9	Discounted by:	22.20%
8	Discounted by:	12.50%
7		
6	Increased by:	16.70%
5	Increased by:	40.00%
4	Increased by:	75.00%
3	Increased by:	133.30%
2	Increased by:	250.00%
1	Increased by:	600.00%

Courtesy ClickEquations Inc.

whole numbers between 1 and 10. In fact, these quality scores aren't linear—for example, the difference between a 7 and an 8 is not equal to the difference between a 9 and a 10.

The chart was made by dividing by the simple whole numbers 1 through 9, but the quality scores that Google divides by when calculating your actual CPC are not simple whole numbers. This means that the table above is wrong.

Due to the differences between visible quality scores and the quality scores used to calculate CPC, the percentages shown *are not* the amount by which CPC is modified by any specific quality score. There is no way to create an accurate version of this table because we don't know the range of numbers used for quality score for CPC or the numeric distance between any two values.

Google appears to use some type of logarithmic or irregular scale. The fact that it's not linear has a dramatic impact on how much CPC goes down when quality score goes up, or how much CPC goes up when quality score goes down. So a quality score of 18.2 might translate into a visible quality score of 6, while an 18.9 might get a visible quality score of 7 and a 24.3 might be necessary to get a visible quality score of 8. The impact on the CPC calculation is obvious. The difference between dividing a number by 18.2 and 18.9 is minor. But the difference between dividing a number by 18.9 and 24.3 is not.

So whatever the real numbers are (and we don't know them), the table above almost certainly exaggerates the impact of most quality score changes on CPC. Increasing quality score will save you money, and drops in quality score will cost you on every click, but Google hasn't yet released enough information to calculate the exact or even approximate size of such changes.

WHEN ADS STAND ALONE

If the calculation of your CPC is based on ads from other advertisers, you might wonder how clicks are priced when you're the only advertiser.

> *In this case, a click costs the lowest price possible for your ad to be eligible to show. This price depends on the matched keyword's Quality Score: the higher the Quality Score, the less you pay, and vice versa.*
>
> Source: http://goo.gl/FXdYm

The answer is that you pay the minimum bid required for that keyword based upon your quality score. The same as the last (lowest positioned) advertiser when there are multiple ads.

Quality Score Impact Four:

The First Page Bid Estimate

The final impact of quality score is its effect on a keyword's first page bid estimate. The first page bid estimate (FPBE) is designed to offer advertisers a clue about what bid a given keyword might need to earn a position on the first page given its current quality score. It may also be a clue about the minimum bid necessary to gain eligibility into auctions for some search queries that match your keyword.

Here's what Google says about the FPBE:

> *On your Keyword Analysis page, you'll see a metric labeled "Estimated bid to show on the first page." This metric, also called the "first page bid estimate," approximates the cost-per-click (CPC) bid needed for your ad to reach the first page of Google search results when the search query exactly matches your keyword. The estimate is based on the quality score and current advertiser competition for that keyword.*
>
> *First page bid estimates are intended to give you greater insight with which to plan your bidding strategy. Meeting your first page bid is not a*

guarantee of placement. Ad placement will still be dependent on quality score, your cost-per-click (CPC) bid, your budget and account settings, and user and advertiser behavior.

Source: http://goo.gl/CD2U8

Another valuable statistic is the first page bid estimate, which is displayed in your account's Ad Group Details pages under the Keywords tab. These estimates show roughly how much you'd have to bid for your keywords to trigger ads on the first page of search results, given their quality scores. This data gives you a much more realistic view of how competitive it is to receive significant amounts of traffic for a keyword.

Source: http://goo.gl/e8g75

While we don't know exactly how Google calculates FPBEs, we might assume they take the bids and quality scores of advertisers who have made it to the first page and use their data to determine, based on your existing quality score, what your bid would have to be to earn an ad rank high enough to appear on the first page.

If you had a quality score of 4, for example, and the eighth placed advertiser in the last auction had an ad rank of 50, then your FPBE would be $12.50; with a bid lower than $12.51 and a quality score of 4, you couldn't earn an ad rank good enough to appear on page 1. Of course, the actual math would use quality score for CPC rather than visible quality score in the calculation.

Remember that landing page quality score is used as a factor in the calculation of FPBE, even though it is not used in the way quality score is used to calculate ad rank. It's hard to say what this means mathematically, but it's a safe bet that if you have a low landing page quality score, you're going to see higher first page bid estimates.

Max. CPC	Est. first page bid
	--
$7.50	$21.00
$9.50	**$17.00**
$4.00	$16.00
$7.50	$16.00
$11.00	**$14.00**
$6.50	**$14.00**

Search query (and, we assume, geography) is not used in the FPBE calculation. Like visible quality score, FPBE is calculated based on the assumption that query is identical to keyword.

> *For calculating first page bid, quality score doesn't consider the matched ad or search query, since this estimate appears as a metric in your account and doesn't vary per search query.*

Source: http://goo.gl/4fvcm

Google says that first page bid estimates are simply feedback rather than a driver of what happens to any particular keyword in any given situation. If the current max CPC for a keyword is lower than its FPBE, the keyword will likely not be eligible for many auctions it could potentially join, so the keyword will probably see a pretty low number of impressions—or at least a much lower number than if the max CPC were closer to or above the FPBE. But when that keyword is ruled ineligible for any particular auction, it is because of the keyword's quality score and not because of the FPBE. And when the keyword is ruled eligible and does earn an impression, it very well could be that the max CPC was below the FPBE but, in that particular situation, the keyword's quality score was good enough to earn the impression. The point is, a low FPBE is a symptom, but low quality score is the real disease.

As such, it's worth mentioning that it's not always necessary to hit the first page bid estimate for the ads associated with your keywords to appear on the first page of the search results. We commonly see keywords with bids below the FPBE get many impressions and clicks, often with good average positions.

This cannot be fully explained. It may reflect the variation in performance based on different search queries or searchers from different geographies, or variations that take place over time based on a changing competitive landscape. Whatever the reason, we recommend that you use the FPBE as one data point among many when deciding your bids or which keywords to prioritize in terms of quality score improvement efforts. Blindly raising bids to meet or exceed the FPBE can cost and waste money. As always, a bit of trial and error is recommended.

Chapter Summary

The quality score assigned to each keyword in your AdWords account drives the success or failure of your paid search campaigns by impacting when and where your ads are displayed and the price you pay for each click.

Quality score is used in four different calculations:

- ◆ **Eligibility**. After someone executes a search, but before Google holds the auction to see which ads appear in which slot, they use quality score to determine which keywords are eligible to enter the auction. Relevant keywords with quality scores below a certain threshold are not included in the auction.

- ◆ **Ad Position**. If your keyword is deemed eligible for an auction, the position it earns is determined by comparing the ad rank of your keyword (ad rank = bid x quality score) to that of other eligible keywords.

- ◆ **Cost Per Click**. Once your position has been determined for a particular search, your CPC is calculated by dividing the ad rank of the advertiser below you by your quality score.

- ◆ **First Page Bid Estimate**. The lower your quality score for a particular keyword, the higher your max CPC (bid) has to be to earn a potential slot on the first page of the search results.

Low quality scores put keywords into an economic death spiral. Their ads appear less frequently (because they fail eligibility requirements), and when they do manage to appear, they'll be matched to generally less competitive search queries with lower conversion potential. Their ads will appear in lower slots on the search results page, and their cost per click will be inflated. This can lead to even lower click-through rates, or to bid reductions due to decreased returns, further accelerating the keyword's decline.

Keywords earning good or great quality scores, on the other hand, gain entry into more auctions, win higher positions, and cost less for every click the receive.

Chapter Seven:
The Numbers and What They Mean

Quality score is deceptively simple. What could be more straightforward than a set of numbers between 1 and 10 where lower is bad and higher is good? Most of us have had a lifetime of experience dealing with things that are graded on a scale of 1 to 10.

But as you've seen thus far, nothing about quality score is simple. The scale doesn't appear to be linear and the distribution isn't normal. The criteria to earn one score or another, or improve a score from one level to the next, are not clear. And while two important impacts of quality score are clear—the way it's used to calculate ad rank and CPC—it isn't precisely clear how the score affects auction eligibility, the setting of first page bid estimates, the display of ad extensions, or other aspects of your campaigns.

This chapter explains everything we do know about what the various quality score levels mean and what they tell you about the keywords to which they're assigned. We also step back from individual keyword quality scores to look at the distribution of quality scores across your account: to see what can be learned about overall account performance and how to approach and track your account-wide quality score management efforts.

Viewing Quality Score

The visible quality score metric of any keyword in your account is displayed or available at least five different ways:

1. **The Keywords Tab in AdWords.** The "Qual. Score" column appears to the right of each keyword in the AdWords interface, listing the current quality score of each keyword as a ratio such as "7/10" (meaning the keyword has a score of 7 out of a possible of 10).

2. **The Status Window in AdWords.** You can also see the quality score of a keyword by hovering over or clicking the "keyword diagnosis" icon (AKA: the thought bubble) that appears in the Status column on the Keywords tab in AdWords. This brings up a small window displaying quality score and offering some feedback about the relevance and landing page quality associated with that keyword.

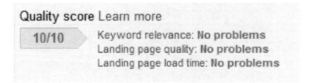

Relevance and landing page feedback is presented as either "Poor" or "No problems." "Poor" status is cause for concern, and almost certainly drives your quality score down substantially. You'll want to take corrective action as soon as possible (using techniques described in *Chapter Eleven: Everyday Quality Score Management*) or pause/delete these keywords, ads, or landing pages.

3. **The AdWords Placement/Keyword Performance Report**. This report includes keyword quality score. To locate it, click on the Reports tab in AdWords, then click "Create a New Report." Select the Placement/Keyword Performance Report, complete the Settings and Options, and click the Create Report button.

4. **The AdWords Editor**. The desktop AdWords Editor displays keyword quality score on each Keyword Tab.

Positives	Negatives	➕ Add Keyword

Keyword	Quality Score
cross-training	3
cross training workout	3
cross training workouts	4
cross fitness training	5
cross-fit 08054	5
crossfit 08054	3
crossfit south jersey	5
cross-fit south jersey	7
cross-training south jersey	7
cross training moorestown	6

5. **The AdWords API**. Google makes an API available for third-party tools or utilities to call for the quality score metric along with other keyword data. In ClickEquations, for example, quality score appears as a column the Keyword Tab, and is available in Excel via ClickEquations Analyst.

What Quality Score Numbers Mean

Quality score is presented in AdWords as a number between 1 and 10. It is sometimes presented in the form of a ratio, such as "7/10," which means that keyword has an average quality score of seven out of a potential of ten.

As detailed earlier, visible quality score is not the actual number used to determine whether a keyword is eligible for an auction, to calculate ad rank, to determine CPC, or to set first page bid estimates. It's an average or approximation of a more complex and changing set of numbers used behind the scenes. The "real" quality score used in calculations is not an integer, is based on keyword/text ad pairs, and is calculated in real time based on the query and geography of the searcher. But visible quality score is all that AdWords shares and is therefore the only information you have to manage your quality scores or report on progress.

Google doesn't say much about what these numbers mean:

> *The number is a finer breakdown of our standard quality scale of "Poor," "Ok," and "Great." On this scale, 1 is the lowest rating, while 10 is the highest. 1–4 corresponds with Poor, 5–7 with OK, and 8–10 with Great.*

Source: http://goo.gl/81Uyq

These are, of course, reasonable definitions, but we think about them a little differently, with a clearer acknowledgement of the special role of quality score 7 and a harsher view of scores 1 through 6.

The table at right shows the scores with our breakdowns and designations. There are four groups instead of three since 7 is alone in the "Good" group, and 1–4 get the more definitive name "Bad."

Below are some extended thoughts on each of these quality scores.

Quality Scores Defined		
Great	10	Perfect
Great	9	Excellent
Great	8	Great
Good	7	Good
Poor	6	OK
Poor	5	Poor
Bad	4	Bad
Bad	3	Terrible
Bad	2	Horrible
Bad	1	Disgusting

QUALITY SCORES 10, 9, AND 8: THE GREAT ONES

Keywords that earn quality scores higher than 7 are technically doing "better than average," but that phrase doesn't really do them justice. In the grand scheme of AdWords, and in terms of the benefits they convey, these quality scores are rare and powerful.

Keywords earn these scores by delivering CTRs significantly higher than AdWords expects based on the performance of other advertisers with identical or similar keywords. Of course, to earn these high quality scores (8, 9, or 10), you also need good relevance, no penalties, and a good account history.

10 Is Outstanding. When a keyword earns a quality score of 10, it has demonstrated the ability to deliver exceptional click-through rates. These keywords then enjoy a lot of impressions, high positions (they often appear on top of the organic listings, as opposed to on the right side of the page), a significant CPC reduction, and other benefits we'll discuss below.

8-9 Are Very Good. These scores reflect above average click-through rates and great relevance. Only a small percentage of all keywords earn these scores, and they too enjoy a lot of impressions, high positions, a significant CPC reduction, and other benefits we'll discuss below.

There's a persistent rumor running around the internets that quality scores of 8 or 9 don't really exist. Rest assured they do exist, and they appear in many accounts, albeit in far lower percentages than any other scores but 1 and 2. We assume that 8s and 9s are rare because most keywords are either average (earning 7s) or blockbusters (earning 10s), and not many are better-than-average but not blockbusters.

More often than not, keywords with these very high quality scores are "brand keywords": keywords that contain specific words and phrases that identify the company or products and direct searchers to the brand owner's official site. Brand searchers are often looking for the official website and therefore click branded keywords in very high percentages.

Non-brand keywords that earn high quality scores have something else driving CTR overachievement. The most common reasons are:

- **Motivated Searchers**. When many of the people searching a particular term or phrase really want a specific result (such as when people are trying to find a specific recipe and your ad promises exactly that recipe), or when a product or topic suddenly generates a lot of action-oriented interest (like when Oprah mentions a product and you happen to be one of the few advertisers who offers it), CTR can be very high.

- **Excellent Ad Copy**. When text ad copy clicks with searchers (pardon the expression), they respond by clicking in greater-than-expected numbers. This usually reflects excellent copywriting that can use one of over a dozen different triggers to connect and persuade.

The Benefits of Excellent Quality Scores

Keywords with great quality scores get important core benefits: more impressions, better positions, and lower CPCs. But high scores also make these ads eligible for other benefits, including top positions, sitelinks, and ad extensions.

It isn't precisely clear what quality score is required for these benefits, and some suggest that only keywords earning 10s can get them. But it seems likely that these benefits are extended to scores of 8 and 9 at least sometimes. The official Google help pages, for example, says that sitelinks require a "very high quality score," but doesn't explicitly say a 10 is required.

Sitelinks will appear for ads with the highest Quality Scores.

Source: http://goo.gl/JCp0e

Let's take a look at the special benefits that keywords with high quality score can enjoy:

♦ **Top position**. Ads that appear above the organic rankings at the top of the results page, as opposed to down the right edge of the page, are chosen in part based on quality score. In some cases, only ads that have earned a quality score of 10 will appear on top, and if none of the ads have earned that score, there will simply be no top-position ads in those search results.

Quality score even enables ads to jump to the top, moving up over ads that earned a higher ad rank. In other words, if your quality score multiplied by your bid earned you the third position in an auction, but your quality score was 10 and the two ads that earned higher ad ranks only had quality scores of 7, then AdWords may choose to move your ad into the top center slot (which is effectively position #1) while leaving the ads with higher ad ranks but lower quality scores on the right edge.

> *A keyword's Quality Score for ad position is based on its click-through rate (CTR) on Google, the relevance of the ad and keyword to the search query, historical keyword performance, and other relevancy factors.*
>
> *For ad placement in top positions above Google search results, we use the same formula, based on your Quality Score and CPC bid. However, only top-ranked ads—ads that exceed a certain Quality Score and CPC bid threshold—are eligible to appear in these positions.*
>
> *The CPC bid threshold is determined by the matched keyword's Quality Score; the higher Quality Score, the lower the CPC threshold. This ensures that quality plays an even more important role in determining the ads that show above search results.*

Source: http://goo.gl/9TU5H

♦ **Sitelinks**. When an ad in one of your campaigns is given "sitelink" status, up to four additional links appear below that ad. You specify the links at the campaign level, so there isn't keyword-specific or ad-specific control, but the extra links, space, and visibility do contribute to much higher CTRs.

The following best practices will help maximize your chances of showing Sitelinks:

- *Your ad should have one of the top positions above the search results.*
- *Your ad should have a very high Quality Score.*
- *Your Sitelinks URLs must direct users to pages that are part of your main website.*

Source: http://goo.gl/xYJQn

♦ **Product Ads and Other AdWords Extensions**. All of the AdWords extensions (at the time of this writing, that includes products, location, phone, video, and seller ratings) are enabled with some consideration of quality score. It isn't clear if a consistent or variable minimum quality threshold is required to have these extensions appear, but they often seem to be available only to keywords with excellent quality scores. (Learn more about AdWords extensions at http://goo.gl/s59vn.)

♦ **Dynamic Keyword Insertion.** Although not exclusively a bonus for keywords with quality scores of 10, dynamic keyword insertions (DKIs) do generally require a quality score of 7 or higher to substitute the search query for the DKI text in your ad copy. DKIs are discussed in more detail in *Chapter Eight: The Simple Path to Good Quality Scores.*

QUALITY SCORE 7: THE STANDARD

Quality score 7 is by far the most common quality score and can be considered a good result. It's easy to do worse and hard to do better. A keyword that has earned a score of 7 has no relevance or landing page problems and has achieved a click-through rate within the bounds that Google believes are normal for that keyword.

Statistically, 7 is the *mode*—the most frequently occurring number of all quality scores across all accounts—although of course it may not be most common quality score in your account.

Should you be satisfied with a quality score of 7? The answer is yes in most cases. The only real exception would be keywords directly related to your brand—they should be able to do better.

While you can certainly work to improve the click-through rates of keywords that have earned a quality score of 7, it's generally very difficult to make the jump into the great quality score range of 8–10.

As we'll elaborate on later in this chapter, it appears that a very significant CTR increase is required to move past quality score 7. There are great benefits to doing so, and no harm in trying, but it'll rarely be worth pulling your hair out if 7 is the best quality score you can achieve on a non-branded keyword.

QUALITY SCORES 6 AND 5: NEARLY GOOD ENOUGH?

Quality scores of 5 and 6 are referred to as "OK" by Google but reflect suboptimal performance in terms of CTR, relevance, or landing page quality. In an ideal world, none of your keywords would earn scores below 7. And in a black-and-white world, any keyword that does earn a score below 7 would be considered sub-par, disadvantageous, and in need of immediate attention or removal.

But in the real world, this isn't true. Google hasn't shared their criteria, grading curve, or real numbers used to impact positions and costs, so we don't really know how far a 6 is from a 7. A 6 is worse than a 7, but we can't be sure if it's a little worse or significantly worse. All we do know is that it isn't as bad as a 5.

Since there are no hard facts about what's "good" and "bad," we're forced to be a little vague in making recommendations. But in our opinion, 6s should be cut some slack, 5s should be put on the rack. No insider information is driving that, just experience and consideration.

A 5 is not almost a 7, so we're comfortable saying that when a keyword earns a 5, something is definitely wrong. Google translates a 5 as "OK," but we don't find this detail compelling enough to consider 5s acceptable. The results are sub-par, and in most cases, significant attention and action are warranted. Keywords with quality scores of 5 or below are detrimental to your results. (We'll talk more about where to draw the line and what those lines mean in later chapters.)

QUALITY SCORES 4, 3, 2, AND 1: THE STINKERS

Scores of 1–4 are *terrible*. Google calls these ratings "poor," but they're much worse than that. Keywords with quality scores this low are very frequently ineligible for auctions, so they don't get many impressions. If they do get impressions, they have a relatively high cost per click because of their low quality scores.

It is possible but somewhat rare to earn these low scores through bad CTR alone. More often, these scores are caused by landing page issues or serious relevance problems, and they'll show as "Poor" in the keyword quality status dialog box.

Low quality scores are Google's way of saying you probably shouldn't be advertising on that keyword. Low quality scores drive down impressions and positions and drive up costs, and the factors that cause some keywords to earn low quality scores can slowly eat away at all the keyword quality scores in your account. There just aren't very many good reasons for allowing low quality score keywords to remain active in your account indefinitely.

It's important to take action on low quality score keywords—even if that action is a decision to live with some of them—because low quality score keywords are bad for all of your results. They almost always lose money themselves, and they can drag down the performance of all the keywords in your account.

How Are Quality Scores Distributed?

When Dr. Siddharth Shah at Efficient Frontier reviewed quality scores across millions of keywords in accounts under their management, they found the following distribution of quality scores:

As you can see, in this group of accounts the vast majority of keywords earned a quality score of 7. A very small percentage earned 8s or 9s, but a respectable 17.83% earned the maximum score of 10. There is a healthy distribution of 5s and 6s, and just over 10% of the keywords in the 1–4 range. This distribution is interesting and instructive—and probably representative of many but not all accounts. This particular concentration of 10s, for example, is likely a bit higher than average due to the fact that Efficient Frontier manages search campaigns for many large and well-known brands who are likely to see huge CTRs on their branded keywords.

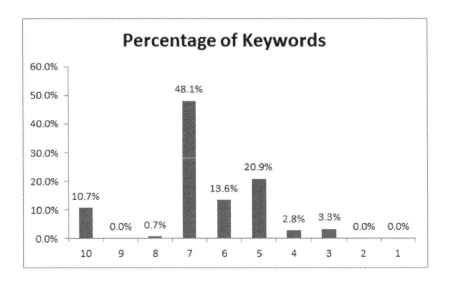

Viewing Account-wide Quality Score Distributions

Even though quality score is reported and managed at the keyword level, it is very helpful to have an account-wide perspective on your quality score as well. This can make it easier to set your initial quality score goals and to drive your quality score management strategy.

A quality score distribution graph shows how the keywords in your account have earned (or been assigned) quality scores from 1 through 10. Strangely, there are no tools within AdWords to help you understand or take action based on the distribution of scores within your account. This means that few PPC managers are taking advantage of this valuable view.

While the exact distribution of quality scores varies for every account, there are common patterns. The three dominant patterns reflect what we'll call great, mixed, and horrible performance in terms of account-wide quality scores, and they're defined by the percentage of keywords that appear in each section of the distribution.

The charts below are based on actual AdWords accounts. Along with each are some initial thoughts on what the shape says about the account from a quality score perspective. In *Chapter Nine: Quality Score Management Basics*, we dive into each of these distribution patterns in much greater detail to review the initial management strategies each suggests.

Note that these charts are based on simple counts of keywords at each quality score level. It is also useful and interesting to produce these charts based on impression-weighted numbers so that the impact of keywords with poor scores but few impressions (or great scores and many impressions) are more clearly reflected.

◆ **An account is in great shape** if it's filled with 10s and 7s and has just a small number (< 25%) of quality scores below 7. In this case, you can take a targeted approach to working on the pesky 5s and 6s in your account, and you probably don't have very many scores below 5.

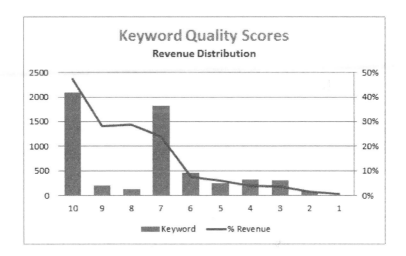

◆ **An account is mixed** if the majority (or near-majority) or your keywords are at or near 7s but you also have a few 10s and a wide distribution of scores between 3 and 6 that account for 25% or more of your keywords. This suggests that you'll have to work very hard and probably reconsider some of the areas where you're trying to advertise.

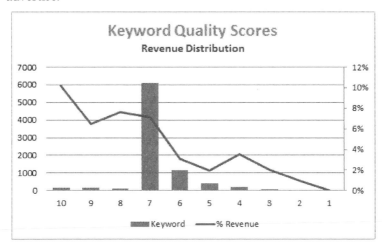

♦ **An account is in horrible shape** if more than 33% of your keywords have quality scores below 6 and there are few or none above 7. You may need to reconsider your approach to paid search and/or take some radical measures to improve these results.

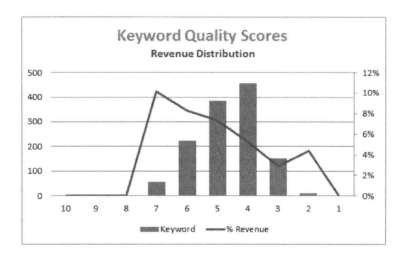

PLOTTING QUALITY SCORE DISTRIBUTION FOR YOUR ACCOUNT

Finding and plotting the distribution of quality scores in your account takes some work. You could simply look at a list of all your keywords and try to eyeball the ratio of 4s to 7s to 10s, but it's not that hard to get a more precise accounting.

If you use ClickEquations, you can run the Quality Score Distribution model report in ClickEquations Analyst. You'll see the number of keywords at each level, as well as the corresponding costs, revenues, and conversions.

If you don't have ClickEquations, you can create your own version of this report in Excel using data from AdWords. All you need is the free Excel template and instructions you can get at http://goo.gl/Ffzml.

How Often Are Quality Scores Updated?

The actual quality score used to impact your account is recalculated every time a search is performed. Visible quality scores as reported by AdWords appear to update every day.

But there is no way to know how often the components that go into that score are updated. For example, Google has made clear that landing page reviews do not happen instantly or sometimes even quickly when target URLs are updated. Nor do they revisit landing pages very frequently to check if they've been changed or improved after a landing page penalty or warning has been issued.

> *Note that any changes to Quality Score will not happen immediately. The AdWords system may take up to a few weeks to reassess the keyword's Quality Score in the context of the ads and landing page in its new ad group. During this time, you may see stronger fluctuations in Quality Score than usual as the system processes the new information.*

> Source: http://goo.gl/24amN

You can most clearly see the change and development of quality scores for new keywords added to your account. An initial quality score is usually assigned very quickly, often before the first impression. As impression and click counts build, the score can change frequently over the first few days and often stabilizes within a week or so, even for keywords with relatively low impressions and clicks.

Chapter Summary

Quality score tells you how efficiently or inefficiently each keyword in your account is being used. With each rating, Google delivers a specific message about how the keyword is performing and how you need to react.

- ◆ **Quality scores of 8, 9, and 10 tell you that the keyword is working exceptionally well**. It's delivering high click-through rates and providing maximum visibility at the lowest possible cost. Your work is done.

- ◆ **A quality score of 7 means a keyword is performing well**. There are no problems that need attention and both coverage and costs are reasonable. You can always work to improve, but no urgency is required.

- ◆ **Quality scores of 5 and 6 suggest both that there is room for improvement and that improvement is possible.** These keywords aren't failing, but they're coming up short. As a result, they're missing impressions and costing more than necessary.

- ◆ **Quality scores of 1, 2, 3, or 4 should appear red and flashing in the AdWords interface**. They're a clear sign of either keyword-level or account-wide problems that must be urgently addressed. If they represent isolated cases in the account, they should almost certainly be paused if they can't be immediately improved.

While individual quality scores matter, you can also learn a lot by considering the collective quality scores of all the keywords in your account. In *Chapter Nine: Quality Score Management Basics*, we'll look at how to review the distribution of quality scores in your account and use these numbers, and a bucketed view of them, to understand the total amount of work and potential for account-wide quality score improvement.

Part III:
Improving Quality Score

Chapter Eight:
The Simple Path
to Good Quality Scores

Before we tackle the difficult work of diagnosing and curing quality score problems, let's look at core principles and practices that can produce good quality scores naturally. These are particularly useful if you have the good fortune of building a new account from scratch, but they're also important to understand as foundational goals when rehabilitating existing accounts.

The goal is to create and manage the account in ways that facilitate high click-through rates, relevance, and good user experiences. There are three principles you'll want to keep in mind:

1. Target only searchers who are likely to be interested in your offer.

2. Make each offer clear, compelling, and persuasive.

3. Fulfill the promise of each ad with a positive post-click experience.

Targeting, clarity, and a positive experience are all subjective measures, but if you apply strict (even bordering on extreme) standards for each, then your keywords will have the pre-requisites they need for good or great quality scores. Stray from strict observance of these principles or work on an account that has, and you'll know just where to begin looking when quality scores are low.

The Quality Way

As we've learned, quality score measures how poised a particular keyword is for success given the way your ad group is organized and configured. The measurement considers past performance and the expectation of future performance, which Google bases on specific attributes that correlate strongly with high CTRs and great results.

As such, when you demonstrate the ability to manage ad groups and add keywords in a way that delivers success, new keywords are rewarded with good initial quality scores. But if your history isn't clear or shows a recurring lack of CTR or other problems, new keywords are punished.

Google knows the old adage, "What gets measured gets done." They measure quality score and tell you (more or less) what they're measuring so that you'll take the actions necessary to improve your scores. It's a direct effort to shape your behavior.

As is clear by now, what quality score measures and how it's done is complex and full of subtleties. Google never really sums up exactly what they want you to do. Our reading is that Google is making four strong suggestions:

1. **Choose keywords that reflect direct interest and intent toward your products or services**. Many keywords or phrases related to your business are highly or entirely unlikely to be searched on by people who are looking for you. Buying keywords that suggest or prove to have specific intent is the first step toward paid search success and good quality scores.

2. **Organize your keywords into tightly focused ad groups**. Logical keyword organization delivers relevance. The way you choose to group keywords directly controls the way in which search queries are matched to text ads. The narrower the range, the higher your chances of success.

3. **Write direct and compelling ad copy**. Your text ads must persuade the users who see them to click. Carefully review the keywords in every ad group and the search queries they attract, and continuously test ad copy to find the best possible click-through rates.

4. **Create clear and effective landing pages.** Searchers should be promised a landing page that fulfills the message of the ad copy, and then once they click they should get not only what they were promised but also what they expected. Target URLs should be informative, and landing pages should be as narrowly focused as possible on the interests and intent implied by your keywords, the search queries they attract, and your ad copy. Making sure that users avoid a poor landing page experience helps you avoid quality score penalties and plays a more important role toward the ultimate goal of conversions.

You may view Google's efforts to influence the management of your account as manipulative and even unfair. They're pushing you to buy certain keywords and avoid others, and they're rewarding you for using certain versions of ad copy while punishing you for others.

But the requirements and requests they make in the name of quality score are in fact doing advertisers a big favor. Quality score notifies you of problems and weaknesses within your account. You can and should use this information to prioritize focus and effort. This can put you at a great advantage over advertisers who ignore these signals.

Most advertisers will find Google's principles perfectly aligned with their own goals and economic interests:

- Every keyword you advertise on should be aimed directly at specific users.

- Every text ad in your account should directly answer whatever question is implicit in the search that displays it.

- Every landing page you take people to should satisfy their desire and deliver on the promise of your ad copy.

Who could argue with these ideals, even if there were no such thing as quality score?

The Quality Score Shortcut

Think of the four rules listed above as a set of best practices that provide the basis for good paid search results and quality scores. Take them to heart and you'll wind up with a well-organized AdWords account filled with intelligently selected and refined keywords, compelling and persuasive ad copy, and informative and appealing landing pages. These steps enable your account to deliver the relevance, click-through rates, and user experience that are the core of what quality score measures.

The following sections look at each of these steps in greater detail.

Step 1: Choose Appropriate Keywords

Keywords are the door through which every paid search prospect must pass. As a marketer, it's almost instinctive to want to reach the maximum number of people by helping any prospect who wants to find you to do so. And so it seems (before you really think about it) that more keywords equals better paid search marketing.

But it isn't true.

In traditional marketing channels, the idea was to get your message in front of as many people as possible and leave the job of qualifying prospects to the sales people. And why not? Marketing costs were usually fixed, so a flat rate fee got your newspaper ad or TV commercial run. You hoped as many people as possible saw the ad and that nearly all of them would respond. Then it was the sales people's turn to sell.

But paid search is different. Every person who clicks on your ad costs you money. It's in your best interest to have only truly qualified prospects click on the ads. Plus, via quality score, AdWords actually punishes you for showing your ads to people who prove uninterested in them.

The first step to ensuring that only the qualified people click your ads is to make sure that only qualified people see your ads. This is done through intelligent and judicious keyword selection and pruning.

The trick is to prioritize quality over quantity when it comes to keywords. Paid search should be practiced with a rifle, not a net. The fact that a keyword is related to your business or the subject domain in which your business operates does not mean that the word or phrase belongs in your account. The vast majority of the keywords in your account should be those you truly expect to attract searchers with clear intent directly related to your products or services. If you aren't selective, and instead add every word, phrase, name, and concept related to the domain or category of your offerings, your results will suffer—definitely in terms of quality score, and probably economically too.

Associating Keywords with Intent

The drive to add as many keywords as possible is strong and prevalent in paid search. You'll have to work (and argue) to avoid filling your account with keywords that don't clearly correlate to specific search intent. If you think about the keywords in your account now, or those you might add in the future, you can classify each into one of three groups in terms of how clearly it predicts searcher intent:

- **Clear intent**. Keywords like "organic dog food discounts" are unambiguous. The people whose search queries will be matched to this keyword are most likely in buying mode for a specific product.

- **Ambiguous intent**. Keywords like "organic dog food" are matched with search queries people frequently use when shopping, but someone might also be researching a medical issue or trying to learn the safe storage life for previously purchased food.

- **No clear intent**. Category-defining keywords like "pet food," and many other general or generic keywords, will be matched with search queries of great diversity, a large percentage of which will clearly have nothing at all to do with buying dog food.

Success is yours to win or lose with keywords that provide clear intent. The impressions they generate are almost all seen by people who would at least consider clicking on your ad if the copy is persuasive enough. But for keywords with ambiguous or no intent at all, some percentage of the time— and possibly even a large majority of the time—you've lost before you've even begun. Your ads will be shown to people who aren't looking for what you're offering, so it's not surprising they'll rarely click and even more rarely convert.

Here we face the paid search marketers' dilemma: one group of keywords offers precise targeting but low volume, and the other offers huge volume but poor targeting. AdWords quality scores and your own desire for ROI pull you to choose targeted keywords. Your boss (or client) and the pressure for more conversions push you toward adding every keyword with even the slightest relationship. What's a girl to do?

Of course, it isn't realistic or possible to run your account only with keywords of clear intent; in the real world, plenty of impression volume and conversion is locked up in generic or vague search queries. So you need to build a collection of keywords that balance the strength of clear intent with the business need for volume.

These decisions are not easy or clear cut. Keywords with no clear intent can attract a lot of clicks and even conversions. Keywords with what appear to be clear intent can fail miserably. Only through diligent effort such as query mining, match type tuning, keyword negatives, trial and error, and constant vigilance will the best results be achieved.

Consider a simple two-step process:

1. **Build a strong core**. Build and anchor your account around keywords directly related to your offering that have very clear intent. Get ad groups with these keywords running and profitably earning quality scores of 7 or higher. If you can't earn good or great quality scores with these keywords, your chances of doing so with less-targeted words and phrases aren't very good.

2. **Expand around the core**. When you've earned both profit and good quality scores with keywords of clear intent, begin adding keywords of ambiguous intent, and then later keywords with no clear intent, to new ad groups within existing campaigns. Use phrase and exact match types, or at least modified broad match types, and a liberal volume of negative keywords to tune and optimize results.

As you expand your campaign with broader and broader keywords, put each new keyword "on probation" and define specific criteria for volume, return, and quality score that they have to accomplish in order to stay active in your account. Don't expect that every related or relevant keyword "belongs" in the account. Many are worth trying, but not all will be worth keeping. When a keyword isn't working, it's not always the ad copy or the bid or some other parameter that has to change. This ignores the most obvious and often-correct solution: maybe the keyword itself just doesn't belong.

Keyword Caveats

Finding, choosing, optimizing, and ultimately passing judgment on keywords is a complicated topic. The balance between relevance, profitability, and volume is difficult to find. And as we've come to expect, nearly every aspect of the system is fluid; seasonality, the actions of competitors, tweaks to Google's algorithms, and other factors can make a keyword profitable one day and unprofitable the next. In other words, there is no simple prescription for defining the right and wrong keywords for your account.

One additional complication to the idea of focusing toward more specific "long tail" keywords to develop a strong base for your account is the fact that when using extremely narrowly targeted keywords, you may experience quality score challenges *because* the keywords are so specific. Hyper-targeted keywords often have little historical or current search volume, and Google may therefore render harsh initial quality score assumptions which drive up costs and reduce impression volumes. We'll discuss this phenomenon in more detail In *Chapter Twelve: Everyday Quality Score Management,* and offer recommendations for managing low-impression-count keywords.

The fact that quality score ties the success of any keyword to the performance of all others in the account complicates decision making. If this weren't true, the entire exercise of choosing and optimizing keywords could focus on the economic return of each keyword, groups of keywords, or even all keywords in the account. The decision would simply be whether the return on investment was "worth it" or not—based on either a simple economic calculation or some broader measure. Keywords that made more money than they cost would be "good," and those that didn't would be "bad."

Taking that view, if an entire ad group full of keywords was profitable, the incentive to prune individual poor performers from the group would be low. But quality score introduces three ways the performance of one keyword can impact the results of others:

1. **The account's historical click-through rate**: Poor performing keywords lower the recent historical CTR average of the account.

2. **The historical click-through rate for target URLs**: Poor performing keywords reduce the CTR history for target URLs that may be used other ad groups

3. **Low landing page quality:** Landing page penalties often impact far more than the specific keyword and ads that point to those pages. One bad apple can spoil, or at least degrade, the whole account-wide bunch.

The fact that under-performing keywords can reduce the effectiveness of otherwise well-performing keywords should strengthen your resolve not to keep poor performing keywords (in terms of quality score *or* economics) alive for very long in your campaigns. There are many things you can do to create an environment where a keyword has the best possible chance to succeed (the rest of this chapter discusses many of them). But once you've done those things, if the keyword is still underperforming, then it's time to give up on it. If you don't you'll suffer not only the waste associated with that keyword, but also exert a collective downward influence (or even spiral) on the account.

STEP 2: ORGANIZE KEYWORDS INTO TIGHTLY FOCUSED AD GROUPS

Once you've got a set of keywords you believe will attract people with a strong interest in your products or services, the next step is to organize those keywords into ad groups in a way that will deliver relevant and compelling ads to each person who sees them.

Every search query matched to any keyword in an ad group is shown one of the ads from that ad group. That means a potentially huge set of search queries, representing a potentially large set of keywords, all resolve to a very few text ads. This is not a recipe for relevance between query and ad copy.

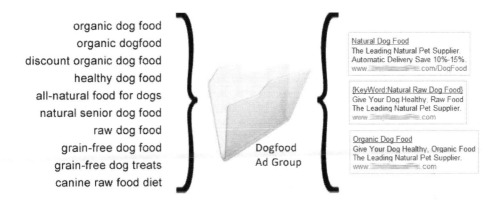

Given these mechanics, the only way to make sure text ads are relevant and compelling to the searchers who see them is to tightly control who can see them in the first place. If all of the keywords in an ad group are tightly focused on a single topic—so much so that they're all effectively synonyms—then every matched search query will have asked nearly the same question and, regardless of which keyword attracted it or which text ad from the group is chosen, the ad copy will be relevant and compelling.

Historically, many ad groups have been built around simple topical groupings filled with all kinds of keywords directly or roughly related to that topic. A pet store might have a campaign for their food products, and within that campaign an ad group for dog food, another for cat food, etc. Text ad copy for such campaigns must be crafted in a somewhat generic fashion so the ads make sense for all the different keywords in that dog food ad group.

Working backward from the ads to the keywords would produce better results. Put a single keyword alone in an ad group and then write the perfect targeted text ad (or several variations) for that keyword. Now add other keywords to the ad group . . . as long as each keyword (and the set of search queries that are likely to be matched to it) is well suited and appropriate for the ad group's text ads.

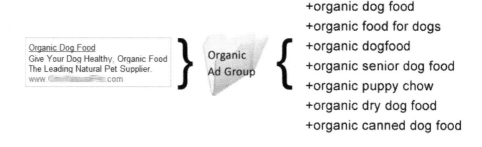

+organic dog food

+organic food for dogs

+organic dogfood

+organic senior dog food

+organic puppy chow

+organic dry dog food

+organic canned dog food

Another option is to organize ad groups around the parts of speech used in the words or phrases in the keywords.

- **Nouns** should usually be separated into different ad groups. Dogs and puppies may both eat that food or use that leash, but the people looking for them are thinking about one or the other.

- **Verbs and adverbs** often reflect the intent, personality, or current/ desired activity of the searcher and can be particularly tough to address with equal effectiveness via a single set of ads. People who want to "order" something are going to click on different ads than those who want to "learn" about something, for example.

- **Adjectives** can be grouped or separated, but if you're grouping a great variety of them (sizes, colors, textures, etc.), then the ad copy should refer to that aspect (such as "20 Colors In Stock").

How Small Is Small Enough?

There are of course limits to how narrow you can make ad groups. There isn't enough time to take everything to its logical conclusion and it's not necessary anyway. If two, ten, or thirty-five keywords are all focused on the same narrow topic and the questions implied in each of them can be answered with the one or more ads, then there is little reason why having them all together in an ad group would negatively impact quality score or business results.

That said, one additional benefit of having a very small number of keywords per ad group is that AdWords bolds any words in the text ad copy that match (or are "similar to") a searcher's query. By dividing keywords into extremely small ad groups, which lets you create custom text ad copy for each, you can produce more situations where the query is in the ad text and therefore bolded more often. Bold words in text ad copy call attention to the ad and often help to increase CTR.

On search sites, part of the ad text appears in bold whenever it matches or nearly matches a user's search query.

Source: http://goo.gl/QxqFv

Based on the way bold ad copy works, some people recommend creating single-keyword ad groups as much as possible. But this extra effort is probably best reserved for your most competitive keywords, high volume/value keywords, and other special circumstances. Even then, there is nothing magical about having only one keyword in the ad group; grouping together variations such as plurals or keyword + modifiers can produce the exact same results in many cases.

STEP 3: WRITE DIRECT AND COMPELLING AD COPY

The copy in your text ads should be highly relevant to the narrow set of keywords and likely search queries that will be matched in their ad group. Producing variations of relevant, compelling, persuasive, and differentiated ad copy in just 95 characters—including body copy and headline—is quite a challenge. It remains more of an art than a science.

The task is easier when working within focused, narrow ad groups. Ad copy can be specific and refer directly to intended actions, characteristics, or other attributes the group targets. Writing for larger and broader keyword sets requires general or generic ad copy to avoid being inappropriate to certain queries; in an effort to talk to everyone, your copy ends up being directly relevant to no one.

Consider the example of keywords related to organic dog food. Users will query all sorts of modifiers: brands (EVO, Wysong), quality (premium, certified), pricing (coupons, discounts), format (dry, canned), age (puppies, older dogs), etc. Adding these specifics to your ad copy enables a direct connection to the searcher that is impossible if the ad must speak to searchers who might be looking for any number of combinations of these attributes.

Keywords in Ad Copy

Including your keywords and phrases in the ad copy is a common "best practice" often shared in discussions of text ads and quality score. Yet the practicality of this depends upon how many keywords—or more accurately, how many root words and phrases—are in the ad group. If three or more synonyms for the same word are in the ad group, it's unlikely that you'll be able to include them all in the ad copy. (If you do, a better approach would be to split them into separate ad groups.)

Including keywords in ad copy demonstrates to the searcher that the ad directly addresses their query. It's reasonable to expect that this will increase CTR in most cases. And since Google then adds emphasis with bold copy if the query is in the ad copy, the odds of gaining attention from the searcher, and their click, increase even further.

But don't feel obligated to include keywords in ad copy just to earn good or great quality scores.

- **It's not the only way to succeed**: Many keywords earn good quality scores—even 10s—without the keyword in the ad copy.

- **Ad copy without keywords can perform well**: There are many clever, interesting, and effective ways to write ad copy that can drive excellent click-through rates and do not rely on literal keyword inclusion. Ad copy that gets higher CTR without the keyword is better than ad copy with the keyword but lower CTR.

- **AdWords does not directly reward ad copy that includes keywords**: Google does not check for the presence of keywords in ad copy, and their inclusion or absence does not directly or automatically improve or reduce quality scores.

Dynamic Keyword Insertion

Most of the same issues and advice described for keywords in ad copy also apply to dynamic keyword insertion (DKI). It's a useful tool that can improve click-through rates, but in many circumstances it's not appropriate, and you can earn great quality scores without it.

DKI takes the keyword that triggers your ad display and inserts it into your ad copy (if it fits). For example, a DKI text ad might look like this:

> *Buy {Keyword:Puppies}*
> *From an Award-Winning Breeder*
> *Satisfaction Guaranteed!*
> *www.Example.com*

In this case, the word "Puppies" could be replaced with a specific breed if the user searched for Poodles, Labs, or Terriers, or the ad would read "Buy Puppies" if the query was too long to fit into the headline. (More on DKI at http://goo.gl/Qim3r.)

> *Well-written keyword insertion ads in well-organized ad groups can make your ads more relevant to users when you use a more general ad with large numbers of keywords. These ads are more likely to receive clicks than a generic ad would for the same ad group. In these cases, keyword insertion may help improve the Quality Scores for your ads and keywords over time through improved click-through rates (CTRs) and overall performance.*

Source: http://goo.gl/anhmR

DKIs can automate relevance between the search query, the keyword, and the ad copy. By putting the user's query in the ad, it looks extremely responsive to their request, which logically could help to earn a click. The risk, of course, is nonsensical headlines that have the opposite effect. DKIs only impact quality score based on their impact on CTR, so they're good if they help CTR and bad if they hurt it.

Cheap **Children**
Never Pay Full Retail Price Again!
Discounts for 20,000+ Stores.
www.RetailMeNot.com

As with the inclusion of keywords in ad copy, we recommend using DKIs only if they're the best option for the ad copy in that situation.

Conclusion

There are many sources for tips and tricks on writing effective ad copy, both online and offline. To learn to write the best and most compelling and clickable ads, we recommend you seek out advice and experience to support your own efforts. In addition to a potentially huge positive impact on quality score, better text ad copy offers the largest bang for your buck in terms of measurable benefits of any area of paid search campaign improvement.

STEP 4: DELIVER A GREAT LANDING PAGE EXPERIENCE

When Google talks about the purpose and goals of quality score, there is always a large focus on the role landing pages play in ensuring a great user experience for searchers. But as the conversation and information gets more specific, the technical role of landing pages seems to diminish and the focus shifts from delivering good experiences to avoiding bad ones.

We think this is the most realistic way to think about landing pages in terms of quality score: they can hurt but they really can't help. A bad landing page can severely reduce quality score, not just for the keywords aimed at that landing page but for your entire account. A "good" landing page, on the other hand, isn't considered in the calculation of landing page quality scores at all.

Your goal should be to avoid quality score landing page penalties and accept the fact that you can't use landing pages to win any quality score points. You should also deliver a good user experience to reduce bounce rates and "short stay" visits which some suggest (but Google will not confirm) are considered as a part of landing page quality score.

The potential negative impact landing pages can have on quality score can be avoided by eliminating trickery or any other content that would negatively impact the experience of your potential customers. That means skipping these all-too-common elements of poor user experience:

- Pop-ups

- Crazy redirects

- Spyware installations,

- Bait-and-switch offers

- Email harvesting

- Slow load times

- Missing privacy policies or contact information

- Browser hijacking

- Any other less-than-noble tactic that might be used to improve "results" for the marketer at the expense of the visitor's privacy or experience.

Beyond the technical aspects of the landing page, landing pages can also expose "policy violations" which may cause Google to stop showing your ads altogether or even ban you as an advertiser. A more detailed discussion of landing page and site quality issues was presented in *Chapter Five: How Quality Score Is Calculated*, and will be discussed again in even more detail in *Chapter 10: Dealing with Disaster*.

Will the Quality Score Shortcut Work?

Quality score is fundamentally driven by click-through rates, as we've learned. Following the four steps described above will help you to build a foundation for quality score success by targeting ads only where success is likely (fish where the fish are), obsessing about relevance in the form of query/ad copy alignment (answer the question), and striving to please with both text ads and landing pages (satisfy the customer). Apply all of these to your campaigns and you'll have high CTRs, near-perfect horizontal and vertical relevance, and a great user experience. With nothing else in the way, these efforts should naturally result in good quality scores.

Will it work every time? No, it won't.

It won't always work because neither your account nor the rules and realities of AdWords are that simple. The choices you'll be forced to make often won't be that straightforward. In some cases, you won't choose the right answer. Your competitors might do diabolical, ingenious, idiotic, and often unexplainable things that will impact your keywords and results. There are facts about keyword and ad performance you can't see because current reporting options hide relevant information. Plus of course, Google has that tiny little asterisk that allows their actions and decisions to be occasionally inconsistent and unexplainable.

In other words, even when you create campaigns and keywords that are structurally built to promote good quality scores, some keywords and even entire ad groups will get low quality scores.

In the next few chapters, we'll learn what to do when this happens in your account.

Chapter Nine:
Preparing to Manage Quality Score

You wake up. You have some coffee or orange juice. You log on. (I know you logged on before the beverage; humor me.) You check your AdWords account. All the quality scores are not 10s. They're not even all 7s.

Despite all your knowledge and all your efforts, your account has not achieved quality score nirvana. What do you do?

There isn't an easy answer. There isn't one reason why any quality score might be lower than you'd like it to be. There isn't even just one thing that any particular quality score number might mean. And there are many possible actions that you could take to try to increase the quality score of any keyword.

To approach this problem effectively, you need a clear goal, a brilliant strategy, a thoughtful perspective, and a proven methodology. Fortunately, we have one of each right here.

Introducing Quality Score Management

Quality score management is the process of reviewing quality scores and reacting to them. You'll seek out and remove or correct anything that may be reducing quality scores, and you'll prioritize changes designed to boost quality scores for as many keywords as possible. Quality score management should become a standard part of your work, just like keyword expansion, bid management, and text-ad copy testing.

Thinking deliberately about quality score at both the account and keyword levels and taking action based on what you find makes it easier to structure and manage your account. Quality score is a powerful technical and moral compass that can guide you through many tough decisions, some of which you might not confront if you don't pay attention to this important metric. And quality score helps you to explain and justify your actions to managers or clients.

At the account level, your quality score distribution can show you the type and amount of work required to improve and provide a sense of accomplishment as you make progress. It can also help you spot and resolve certain kinds of problems that may go unnoticed if you only think about quality score on a keyword-by-keyword basis.

At the individual keyword level, especially when account-wide issues have been resolved, quality score management is a straightforward problem-solving exercise. For any keyword's quality score, there is a list of potential issues, a way to prioritize that list, and specific actions that typically fix or improve each issue. With experience, you'll be able to assess the various factors quickly and know how each can best be addressed.

Before getting to work on your account's quality score management, there are five things you should know or have in place:

1. A view of the **quality score performance across the entire account**.

2. Clear **goals for quality score** in the account.

3. An understanding of **why your quality scores** might be low.

4. Perspective on the **role of each keyword** relative to its score.

5. **Principles** that you've decided to follow when managing quality score.

When you have these five things in place, you can manage quality score. The rest of this chapter is devoted to helping you get them. Then, in chapters ten and eleven, we'll look at putting the system into action.

An Account-wide View: Quality Score Bucket Analysis

Chapter Seven: The Numbers and What They Mean introduced quality score distribution graphs as a convenient way to see all of the scores in your account and get a sense of relative performance. We featured three common distribution patterns: a "great shape" pattern found in accounts with scores primarily at 7 or higher and fewer than 25% at 6 or below; a "mixed" pattern with few 10s, many 7s, and 25% or more of the keywords at 6 or below; and a "horrible" pattern with few 7s and at least 33% of keywords (and often many more) at 6 or below.

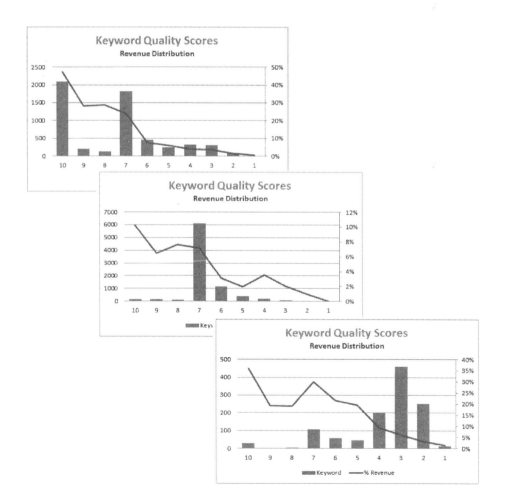

These patterns are extremely common because paid search managers tend to be either highly skilled or not very skilled, and accounts either have account-wide penalties or they don't. Well-constructed and managed accounts usually earn mostly good to great quality scores and rarely have account-wide penalties. On the other hand, it's effectively impossible to earn any (let alone many) very high quality scores in penalized accounts. And accounts that aren't super well-managed but don't have any penalties frequently have lots of 7s, only a few 10s, and a concerning (if not scary) tail of keywords in the 4, 5, and 6 range.

Which is precisely the point: a broad look at quality scores across your account provides a strong indication of both the current state of the account and the positive or negative attributes of the account. You can approach an account differently and rely on a different set of assumptions if the account's overall quality scores are great as opposed to horrible.

Rather they eyeballing distribution bar charts, a great way to look at this data, measure performance, and track accomplishments over time is to bucket keywords by quality score levels or ranges. A bucket analysis shows the percentage of keywords with low versus high quality scores, and makes it easier to gain perspective on your results.

You can use two or three buckets for the analysis. If you divide your keywords into two buckets, one tracks keywords with "good" quality scores and the other those with "bad" quality scores. In the example below, the top group holds keywords with quality scores of 6 through 10, and the bottom one contains only keywords with quality scores of 1 through 5.

QS Distribution Analysis

	Count	%	Spend	%	Revenue	%	Clicks	%
QS = 6-10	1,215	56.7%	$ 9,993	56.3%	$ 130,388	89.3%	12,003	78.7%
QS = 1-5	926	43.3%	$ 7,769	43.7%	$ 15,621	10.7%	3,252	21.3%
	2,141	100.0%	$ 17,761	100.0%	$ 146,009	100.0%	15,255	100.0%

This analysis paints a stark and compelling picture. Keywords with poor quality scores consume over half the account's expense (44%) while providing only 10.7% of the revenue. Moreover, the poor keywords returned 6X less (ROAS is 1304% for the good scoring keywords but only 201% for the poor ones).

Creating three groups (good, poor, and terrible) instead of two provides additional clarity. In the modified version of the table below, you can see we've placed quality scores of 7–10 in the top group, quality scores of 5 and 6 in the second group, and quality scores of 4 or lower in the last group

QS Distribution Analysis

	Count	%	Spend	%	Revenue	%	Clicks	%
QS = 7-10	913	42.6%	$ 8,342	47.0%	$ 117,748	80.6%	10,887	71.4%
QS = 5-6	557	26.0%	$ 4,022	22.6%	$ 18,187	12.5%	2,104	13.8%
QS = 1-4	671	31.3%	$ 5,398	30.4%	$ 10,074	6.9%	2,264	14.8%
	2,141	100.0%	$ 17,761	100.0%	$ 146,009	100.0%	15,255	100.0%

Grouping keywords this way accentuates the fact that the worst performing keywords in terms of quality score are also the worst performing economically. The lowest tier contains 31.3% of the keywords but is responsible for only 6.9% of the revenue while consuming 30.4% of the expense. This is somewhat typical performance for keywords with very low quality scores.

As these examples illustrate, the keywords in your lowest bucket(s) generally do a lot of damage to your results. Improving or pausing these low quality score keywords can have a huge impact on your account and should generally be a priority for any paid search manager.

- Pausing all keywords with quality scores of 4 or less in this example would save $5,398 in one month and increase ROI by 277%.

- Removing these keywords, which likely have very low CTRs, would also help the quality scores of the good and great keywords in the account by increasing (over time) the account's historical average lifetime CTR.

- Improving the quality scores of these keywords, of course, would have even better long terms results than disabling them, as that would deliver incremental sales volume at (hopefully) profitable levels.

The point here, however, isn't which action to take or how to accomplish it, but rather that quality score bucket analysis is a powerful way of analyzing your account and one that frequently reveals important priorities and huge opportunities.

Goals for Quality Score

Once you know where you are, you can decide where you'd like to be. The perfect AdWords account would have quality scores of 7 or higher for every keyword and a healthy set (perhaps 20%) of 10s.

But most accounts are far from perfect, so more realistic goals are probably in order. As a starting point, consider the following targets:

- **Short Term**: Keywords with a quality score of 5 or lower should account for fewer than 35% of your keywords and fewer than 25% of your spending.

- **Long Term**: Keywords with a quality score of 6 or lower should account for fewer than 30% of your keywords and fewer than 20% of your spending. All keywords with quality scores below 5 are either put into "PPC Rehab" or paused/deleted.

These are simply guidelines. The larger your account, the lower the percentage of low-scoring keywords you may want to tolerate. It's also reasonable to take into account the number of impressions for each keyword and strive to have low quality score keywords account for fewer than 10% of the impressions in your account. This assures that they'll be small in number and small in terms of impact on your account CTR history.

It's hard to set goals for quality scores above 7. These scores are highly desirable, and of course you'll do everything possible to earn them, but success isn't entirely in your control. These great results depend a lot on your business segment, user click patterns, and the actions of your competitors.

If you have a recognized brand that gets a lot of search query activity, then it's reasonable to expect to achieve quality scores of 10 on your core brand keywords. Beyond that, 10s are an accomplishment or a gift.

You can, however, set quality score goals for each bucket in order to frame the decision making you'll face and to measure your progress over the weeks and months ahead. Clear, written quality score goals that everyone involved in the account understands will help to guide decisions and simplify communications. These goals should be reviewed and revised at least two if not four times per year to account for changes in the marketplace and as a reality check on your progress.

ABOUT GENERALIZATIONS AND CATEGORIZATIONS

Many of the ideas and suggestions in this chapter include value judgments and action recommendations for situations in which quality scores or percentages are over or under a specific value. These trigger levels and values are approximations only and should not be considered definitive. There are simply too many variables. 25% may be unacceptable in one situation, and fine in another. One keyword with huge impression volume and a quality score of 4 is far worse than 100 keywords with almost no impressions and a quality score of 8. So assume that every numeric line in the sand and their resulting characterizations all have an invisible asterisk next to them that means "Except in your case it might be different."

To put in another way: you are required to supply your own context before accepting, modifying, or rejecting any statements in this chapter (or this book, for that matter).

Why Quality Scores Are Low

Every AdWords account has a range of quality scores, and it's not at all unusual to have some low and even very low quality score keywords. Hopefully, after reading this far, you have a good idea of which basic principles of quality-score-friendly account design may be causing issues in your account.

The root problems or issues most often responsible for low quality scores can be divided into four buckets:

a. **Account or Landing Page Penalties**. A number of account-wide issues can severely reduce quality scores regardless of your click-through rates. These include very low historical account-wide CTRs, landing page penalties, and other issues. These problems and their solutions are discussed in *Chapter Ten: Dealing with Disaster*.

b. **Structural or Technical Problems**. These are the most common causes of low quality scores: poor keyword selection (too generic, mostly), weak organization (too many keywords per ad group), ineffective ad copy (generic or uninteresting), or unacceptable landing pages (that violate AdWords guidelines). These are problems that simply require knowledge and effort to correct.

c. **Keyword Selection**. Sometimes the central structure and content in an account is good, but some of the keyword choices or past work in keyword expansion are inappropriate or just naturally earn low click-through rates. Often this happens with keywords that are technically or theoretically relevant to your products or services but are general or broad terms that have many (rather than one precise) meanings. Such keywords have poor horizontal relevance as discussed in *Chapter Five: How Quality Score Is Calculated*.

d. **Competitive**. Some market segments in AdWords are dominated by fiercely competitive and extremely capable paid search marketers. When your competitors are running highly optimized keywords and ads with great CTRs that are the result of skill, hard work, and lots of trial and error, it can be extremely difficult for a newcomer to break in to the category. Such keywords can earn high quality scores, but not easily and often not quickly.

By understanding the different issues that drive low quality scores, you can equip yourself with a plan of attack and a set of expectations for what that plan will deliver.

Resolving Structural Problems

If structural and technical problems are at the root of your poor quality scores, then the work you need to do is straightforward. The general philosophies laid out in *Chapter Seven: The Simple Path to Good Quality Score*, and the detailed steps included in *Chapter Eleven: Everyday Quality Score Management* will help you to improve your keyword selection, organizational structure, ad copy, and (if necessary) landing pages to set the stage for healthier quality scores.

Resolving Keyword Issues or Overexpansion

If the problem in the account isn't so much a lack of good quality scores as it is an overabundance of poor ones—an important distinction, since the presence of good quality scores helps to rule out some of an account's more severe potential structural problems—then quite a bit of your work may involve pausing or deleting inappropriate or underperforming keywords. In some cases this will be temporary, but in many cases it will be permanent.

Of course, sometimes keywords that earn low quality scores also drive a high volume of business or are extremely profitable. In these cases, you'll probably want to keep the keyword despite its quality score, and that's a fine and rational decision. (See *Keyword Perspectives* later in this chapter for more thoughts on how to consider the role and results of any keyword before taking action.)

But assuming you're not dealing only with profitable or successful keywords that happen to have low quality scores, the trick to reducing your keyword count is usually finding the nerve and the authority to pause a large number of keywords. Everyone associated with the account will have to live with the ramifications of these decisions: there will be a lack of ad presence in some desired areas, impression and click volumes will drop, and the result will likely include lower top-line revenue. On the positive side, you'll have better ROAS/ROI, and the account will be getting healthier rather than sicker.

Pausing all unprofitable keywords with quality scores below 5 is the first logical step in a troubled account. Limit the number of exceptions, and work hard to strengthen and improve keywords that can't be paused or are already doing reasonably well. The goal is to run the account as close to "winners only" as possible to create a new strong base upon which to build future expansion.

You may wish to move paused keywords into a paused "Rehab Later" campaign and sub-accounts. Corrective actions and additional effort may very well help these keywords achieve better quality scores. At the appropriate time, and after applying the techniques detailed in this and the next few chapters, that's a worthwhile effort.

Working in Competitive Markets

When the competitive nature of your market or other external factors drive low quality scores—even when the account is well-designed—the problem is much harder to address. Most AdWords markets are competitive in the sense that many advertisers are competing for relatively few slots on the pages. But few markets are full of good or even great AdWords advertisers with tightly tuned accounts, proven ad copy, high CTRs, and good quality scores.

Life in these segments is radically different than it is for the typical AdWords advertiser. Breaking into them, or going from the back to the front of the pack, requires a good strategy, some patience, and the ability to perform. The fundamentals and goals are the same, but a higher level of execution is required. Strategically, the best approach is to break in from the edges. Start with longer, more specific, more vertical (perhaps geographic) keywords on phrase or even exact match. Find the ad copy strategies that work and prove (to yourself and to Google) that you can earn clicks and good quality scores. Slowly—really S-L-O-W-L-Y—add more keywords only after you've proven success over the course of hundreds of clicks. Don't rush to the broad category terms; move in one step at a time.

It should take weeks and could take many months to both build a track record of success and learn the nuances of what works and what doesn't in terms of the keywords, ad copy, landing pages, and perhaps bid strategies necessary to live and win in a tough market. (This also suggests that you should study the ads and tactics of the successful advertisers in the space even more closely than normal.)

Head Scratchers

It seems that most accounts have more than a few keywords with very low quality scores that don't seem to make any sense in the known context of performance. Most paid search managers have come to accept that there are exceptions to just about every rule and recommendation—and quality scores are clearly no exception.

When the quality score of any particular keyword doesn't make sense, remember that you're working off the best information you have: visible quality score, keyword aggregate CTRs, and almost no visibility into geographic effects, to name a few. There are issues that the data you're allowed to see can't reveal. It's also possible Google is just doing something wacky.

Unless it's a particularly important keyword and the unexpected behavior or results continue for weeks or months on end, it's a good mental-health practice to allow a few crazy-low scores (assuming they're really not caused by anything within your control) to remain active in your account without going nuts over them.

Keyword Perspectives

Account-wide quality score distribution graphs, quality score bucket analyses, and broad quality score goals are all helpful in providing a forest-level perspective to an issue that is almost always considered on a tree-by-tree basis.

But the keywords (trees) must be considered too. Each has important individual characteristics and you shouldn't lose sight of those in your forest-level decision making. The fact is that quality score is just one attribute of a keyword, and before making the decision to change that keyword in any way, you'll want to consider a number its attributes—both the objective metrics and some of the subjective elements, too.

Here's an initial list of questions and topics that should color the decisions you ultimately make in the quality score management process.

- **Is this keyword profitable?** There is no more important question than whether or not a keyword is making money. A profitable keyword with a terrible quality score is still a profitable keyword. An unprofitable keyword with a great quality score is still an unprofitable keyword. Profitability should take margin or cost of goods into account (if possible) and ideally apply a revenue attribution method more sophisticated than the default "last click" method.

- **Is this keyword successful?** Profit isn't the only success metric, and based on your business, all success metrics—new visitors, length of stay on site, and other conversion events like video starts or whitepaper downloads—should be taken into account. Long lead-time B2B purchases have particularly different success metrics, and if that's your business, then that's the way to measure and react.

- **What role does the keyword play?** Every keyword in an account is not of equal importance to the business. Some are critical, some are trivial, and many fall somewhere in between. This idea is tied to that of alternate success metrics, as some keywords serve to recruit new clients, others work during the research or product comparison phase of the buying cycle, and others tend to do the job of "closing." Roles and associated metrics for any keyword should weigh heavily on how you manage that keyword.

- **How many impressions is it getting?** In an account that sees six million impressions per month, there is little urgency to take action on a keyword with thirty impressions a week, regardless of its quality score. On the other hand, a single keyword that sees 150,000 impressions a week should have any low quality score problems addressed as quickly as possible, regardless of the account size.

- **How many impressions has it had thus far?** There is a grave danger in PPC of making decisions based on too little data. Keywords with too few impressions, too diverse a set of user queries or geographies, new or poorly matched ad copy, or a host of other factors do not provide sufficient data to make good, let alone permanent or important, decisions.

  Google has suggested that it could take up to 1,000 impressions to stabilize the quality score of some keywords. Keywords they've seen before from other advertisers may stabilize far more quickly. It would be wise to wait for at least a few hundred impressions before being too sure about the quality score of any new keywords in your account.

- **Has it been positioned for success?** If a keyword lives in an ad group where it doesn't belong, or in an ad group that has had particularly terrible ad copy running, or was running against landing pages marked as "poor," or was in position 13 for the last month, then the current quality score isn't doing any more than confirming that the keyword never really had a chance.

- **Is this one a priority?** There are only so many hours available for managing paid search, let alone for quality score management. As with all other PPC tasks, prioritization is key—which makes understanding which variables drive urgency even more important. For practical reasons, you'll often have to leave less serious problems (keywords with lower spend and lower impressions) unattended for days, weeks, or even months.

Your answers to these questions for any keyword in your account should play a very important part in any decision you make about managing that keyword. **If a keyword is producing significant benefit for your business— leads, sales, or even awareness in some cases—then it probably makes a lot of sense to keep the keyword active in your account, even if it's earning a low quality score**.

The CTR metric that drives quality score is a perfect and direct indicator of how much money Google makes from that keyword. And while it's often a very good indicator of how you fare as an advertiser, it's an indirect measure at best unless page views are your only goal. If you have keywords getting low CTRs, but they're profitable or driving other success metrics for your business, then you can't react as if quality score is the only metric that matters.

This is important. The assumption throughout this book has been that quality score and CTR are good proxies for your business or economic success, but that's not always the case. *Whenever it's not true for your account, and you can find success or benefit despite low quality scores or poor CTR, you should modify your actions accordingly.* If this occurs, it makes sense to create an "exception list" of keywords that you continue to run and make bidding decisions about, despite their low quality scores.

If possible, move these keywords into their own campaign and ad groups to segregate them from the rest of your account. If it's a large number of keywords (more than 5% of the account, for example) you may want to consider moving them into their own AdWords account. *See Chapter 10: Dealing with Disaster* for more information about using more than one AdWords account as a quality score management strategy.

KEYWORD OPTIONS

There are four ways you can respond to an individual keyword based on quality score:

- **Leave it**. Accept the current quality score and make no direct changes. The impact of the quality, and probably the results of the keyword, will remain unchanged.

- **Kill it**. Pause or delete the keyword to stop spending money on it and eliminate any negative effect it's having on the account. Note that there is no functional difference between pausing and deleting a keyword.

- **Fix it**. After analyzing a keyword, you can take some action in attempt to improve its quality score. The performance and results may improve over time.

- **Argue about it**. Particularly if you suspect (or know) that there are (or were) landing page or business model issues connected with your account, you may have to contact Google to attempt to get the account back in their good graces.

These seem like simple choices. But they make it sound like a one-dimensional policy is all you'll need: leave the good ones, kill the bad ones, fix the poor ones, and argue about anywhere you're being treated unfairly.

Of course, in the real world, the choices aren't that simple at all.

The qualitative definitions ("good" and "bad") aren't absolute and have to be considered in context. It's easy to pause all the keywords with a quality score of 5 if your account is full of keywords with a quality score of 7, but if 5s and 6s are all you've got, then you face a much harder decision. It's also important to consider resource limitations; there may be a lot of quality score issues you'd like to fix, but only time to work on a small percentage of them.

Quality Score Management Principles

Once you understand the range of quality scores in your account and have set goals, you can build a matrix of quality score management principles or policies.

These can be implemented as strict rules, or better yet, as guidelines tempered by the progress toward your goals and perspectives on the keywords in your account. Below is an example of a quality score management matrix based simply on the profitability and current quality score of any given keyword.

Keyword	Leave It	Kill It	Fix It
Profitable	QS greater than 4. Fix it when you can.	QS less than 4 (or 5), not mission critical, with large number of impressions, not time to fix.	QS less than 6 and mission critical with large impression volume.
Unprofitable	QS greater than 3 with low impression volume, particularly if mission critical.	QS less than 5 (or 6) and not mission critical, medium to high impression volume.	Mission critical keyword with significant impression volume.

Once you've developed your own matrix, it's fairly straightforward to identify the keywords in each segment using simple saved filters. Taking the matrix above, for example, here's how you could search, sort, and act to execute within your account:

Kill Unprofitable Keywords with Low QS

- **Find**: All keywords where ROI (or ROAS) < target and QS < 5 (or 6).

- **Sort:** By impressions descending.

- **Act**: Pause or delete all non–mission critical keywords. The higher the impression count, the more important it is that you take action.

Kill Profitable Keywords with Low QS

- **Find**: All keywords where ROI (or ROAS) > target and QS < 4 (or 5).

- **Sort:** By impressions descending.

- **Act**: Pause or delete all non–mission critical keywords. The higher the impression count, the more important it is that you take action.

Fix Mission-critical Keywords with Low QS and Meaningful Impression Volume

- **Find**: All keywords where ROI (or ROAS) > target, QS < 6, and impressions > 500. *(Set a low impression count appropriate for your account.)*

- **Sort:** By quality score ascending.

- **Act**: Execute the quality score rehab techniques described in *Chapter Ten: Dealing with Disaster.*

Chapter Summary

To turn quality score management into a core component of your paid search management effort, it helps to build some structure around the process.

Begin by taking an account-wide view of your quality score results. The pattern that emerges from Quality Score Bucket Analysis usually tells you a lot about the condition of both the general account and the account aspects that drive individual keyword-level quality scores. As we'll see in the next chapter, this broad view can drive much of your initial strategy for improving quality score.

Taking this broad view also lets you establish goals and create perspectives from which you can define loose (or tight) policies regarding the general approach you'll take with certain quality score results. Requirements vary, but your long-term goal should, at most, be no more than 30% of keywords with quality scores of 6 or less, and fewer than 20% at 4 or lower.

A small number of root causes may be to blame for low quality scores. If the account isn't being penalized (more on this in the next chapter) or facing fierce competition, then there are structural issues (such as ad group organization or text ad quality), or they keywords you're buying just might not be appropriate for what you're selling.

Not all low quality scores indicate that the keyword should be fixed or killed, and we reviewed a number of issues that should be considered before taking any action. If the keyword is making money or helping your business, then it's a good keyword, regardless of its quality score.

Lastly, this chapter presented a matrix of conditions and actions that you can follow to guide quality score management efforts within your account.

Chapter Ten:
Dealing with Disaster
(When Quality Scores Are Horrible)

The first look at your quality score distribution graphs is often a sobering event. You may have never paid close attention to your quality scores, or perhaps you've just never taken the time to put any individual score in perspective. What many realize for the first time is that their account has a very serious problem: horrible quality scores.

The precise definition of "horrible" almost doesn't matter. When a large number of your keywords have quality scores below 7 (> 33%) and many (20%) are below 5, your account has a serious problem. But any mass of quality scores below 7 and certainly below 5 is not good. Numbers like that are Google telling you in no uncertain terms that you're wasting your money and disappointing their searchers.

Perhaps worse, they've learned not to trust you; they expect that new keywords and text ads will fail, and they make it very hard for you to prove them wrong.

The fact that so many keywords in an account have quality scores below 7 is in itself a problem. But the "horrible" designation is really earned by the keywords with scores below 5. Quality scores below 5 just aren't seen very often in healthy, stable, successful accounts.

The presence of such low scores, particularly more than just a handful, usually indicates that one of these four things is true:

1. **Google hates your business model.** They think you and everyone like you are scammers and scumbags. They'd prefer it if you would give up and close your account. They may even do it for you.

2. **Google doesn't like some or all of your landing pages.** The fastest way to a quality score of 1, 2, or 3 is a landing page penalty.

3. **One or both of the above were true in the past even if they aren't anymore,** but the stench has not yet passed. Google may have not noticed that you've left the dark side.

4. **Your AdWords account sucks.** Without an overriding problem like bad business practices or deceptive landing pages, the only way to get so many uber-low quality scores is to actually earn them with very low click-through rates and extremely weak relevance.

If the problem is one of the first three (a penalty on the account related to business model or landing page issues), then there's really no point in doing much else until you resolve those issues. Working on anything else first is likely to be effort thwarted and wasted. In the next few sections, we'll look at how to address these issues, and then we'll discuss the relatively simpler issue of fixing a non-penalized, just-poor account.

Overcoming Business Model Penalties

Google wants to sell ads to advertisers and marketers who offer legitimately valuable goods or services to interested customers. They don't want to sell ads to those who don't add value (most affiliates), who work in disreputable business segments, or who use suspect business practices.

When Google believes an advertiser fits into one of these categories, they apply penalties to the account, and quality score is often the first and only evidence. There is not, strictly speaking, a "business segment" or "business model" or "business practices" quality score, but using whatever evidence or inference they have, Google does make it difficult or impossible for certain advertisers to participate successfully in AdWords.

The affiliate business model started on the internet with noble intentions and noble practitioners. People and companies who had traffic based on original and valuable content were offered referral fees by merchants who had products or services that the people visiting the site might appreciate. Over time, in many cases, the "original and valuable content" component, and sometimes even the "website" component, disappeared and the affiliate industry became filled with people attempting to jump into the middle of already destined transactions or use various hard-sell techniques to push people into buying often-questionable goods and services.

There are too many unsavory business practices to name—from pop-ups, which are simply annoying, to full-blooded fraud and deceptions that are financially harmful or worse. Google doesn't want to be the conduit to this experience for their search customers. While Google mostly looks for direct evidence of these bad behaviors, they do sometimes simply anticipate them. Call it "business model profiling." If you're selling Viagra, expect to be presumed guilty. The same goes for a lot of other medical, pseudo-medical (read: "diet" or "hair loss" or "male enhancement"), and financial products.

> *Please be aware that some websites may always experience lower Quality Scores due to the nature of the site's content. In these cases, such sites may be unable to further improve their existing Quality Scores.*
>
> Source: http://goo.gl/G4RF4

Google often makes these decisions and assumptions algorithmically, although sometimes human reviewers are involved. Sometimes they paint with a broad brush. It is possible for completely legitimate businesses to be suspected, punished, and end up extremely frustrated with or even defeated by the process.

Some advice if your intentions or HTML are not pure:

- If you work in a market considered disreputable or filled with players who push the limits, expect trouble. This means that if you're telling people how rich they can get by sending you money, if you're selling a pill or a cream or a magnet or some other miracle cure, if you're an affiliate who doesn't offer *huge* amounts of original and useful content, or if you're in a business you wouldn't be proud to describe to everyone you meet, then just do everyone a favor and forget about AdWords.

- If your goal is to collect email addresses, redirect or confuse visitors, install anything, or otherwise manipulate anyone or anything, then expect a lot of trouble.

- If your business segment, business model, or business practices are frowned upon by Google and cannot be changed, give up. There are plenty of online advertising channels that relish their role as the seedy underbelly of commerce. Spend your money there.

- If your account or website (domain) has employed any practices on the no-no list in the past—even by marketers, consultants, or owners who are long gone—you'll still have problems and may or may not be able to clear them up.

Repent and Recover

If your business was guilty but has cleaned up its act, if your business is the rare good guy in a pond full of scum and has been unfairly punished, or if your business is somehow close to one that is often trouble but isn't trouble itself, then with some patience and effort you may be able to get into Google's good graces.

To do so, follow this three-step process:

1. **Make sure your business is REALLY clean**. Your business segment, business model, and business practices must be entirely legitimate according to the standards Google has set. You won't be able to finesse it. There are legitimate businesses in financial, pharmaceutical, affiliate, and other areas that often have trouble, but you'll have to prove to Google that you're the good kind.

2. **Make sure your site is REALLY clean**. Your site, which is your representative on this matter, needs to be exemplary. Make sure every line of content is original, the HTML is clean in every way possible, the privacy policy and about us pages are clear, contact information is clearly provided, and the site is otherwise free of anything that might raise a flag.

3. **Contact Google**. See the Requesting Forgiveness section later in this chapter for details on how to contact Google, what to say, and what to do next.

Note that there is no guarantee you'll be able to correct this problem. The decisions and policies of Google are unilateral and final.

Resolving Landing Page Penalties

The good thing about landing page penalties is how easy it is to know if they're affecting your quality scores. If they are, your keyword status dialog box will say "Landing Page: Poor."

If it says "OK," then you do not have a landing page problem, at least on that keyword. If it says "Poor," you have a problem. You may not believe you deserve this rating—and perhaps you're right—but Google says you have an issue and so you have an issue.

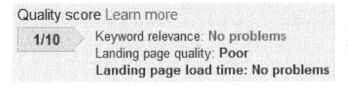

It's unfortunate that the only way to find these "Poor" landing page flags is by manually reviewing the pop-up dialog boxes in AdWords. There is no summary report, and the data is not available via the API. (If it were, third-party tools could more easily make you aware of this dire situation.)

The process for resolving landing page penalties is essentially the same as that described above in regard to clearing up business model and related penalties. You must:

1. Get clean (or verify compliance).

2. Formally request forgiveness from Google.

3. Wait.

Getting Clean / Verifying compliance

Chapter 5: How Quality Score Is Calculated includes the current (at the time of this writing) AdWords rules and restrictions regarding landing page penalties. Review these carefully and make 1,000% sure your site is in compliance both in letter and in spirit.

When explaining poor landing page quality scores to those who contact them about it, Google offers this list of reasons:

- *Sites which offer little to no unique value or functionality.*
- *Sites that show users more ads than content.*
- *Sites with the primary purpose of driving traffic to other sites with a different domain.*
- *Sites that offer no additional value because they copy or mirror all or most of their content from another site.*
- *Shopping aggregators that offer only one to three merchants to compare from. Additionally, many of these merchants are shopping aggregators themselves.*
- *Data collection sites that offer free items or other incentives to collect users' personal information.*
- *Sites that try to trick users into revealing personal information by appearing to be from a legitimate source (e.g. banks or credit card issuers).*
- *Sites that promote outrageous claims about easily making a lot of money with low risk and minimal effort.*
- *Sites that distribute malicious or harmful software to users through downloads or other sources.*
- *Sites that hide billing terms and conditions or aim to deceive users on pricing or billing.*
- *Sites that make inaccurate or misleading claims regarding the product being promoted.*
- *Site that promote low-quality affiliate advertisements or the sale of free items.*

> • *Sites that promote selling counterfeit goods, attempt to deceive consumers into believing the counterfeit is a genuine product of the brand owner, or sell their goods as faux, replicas, imitations, or clones of the original product.*

Source: http://goo.gl/qkl19

There are even more detailed lists of issues and problem examples at http://goo.gl/TEvz3. Click "Ad Visibility Approvals & Performance," then "Ad Approvals and Policies," and finally "Landing page and site policy guidelines." You'll see a long list of links to the detailed policies of over a dozen issues that can result in landing page penalties or more severe ramifications.

Rigorously review these guidelines and examples to understand why your pages were flagged. It is possible but unlikely that your pages were flagged mistakenly. It's far more likely that Google's review algorithms (or people) found something that made them believe or suspect that one of the problems listed above exist in your account. Your best bet is to understand the problem or perception and take complete corrective action before moving forward.

The AdWords Help Forums are often the site of impassioned pleas from people who find their landing pages rated "Poor." Most are confused about why, and more often than not the reason is that their sites are what Google refers to as "low quality affiliate sites whose primary purpose is to send users to another site." If your site is in the affiliate business (or one of the other questionable businesses discussed earlier in this chapter), don't be surprised if your landing pages are ranked Poor. In fact, you should probably consider it a miracle if they're not. Once tagged as Poor and identified as an affiliate site, the chances of correcting the problem and having the penalties lifted are very low.

REQUESTING FORGIVENESS: CONTACTING GOOGLE

When you have identified and corrected every actual or possible violation of the AdWords policies, or are 100% convinced that there never were any actual or possible violations, you can reach out to Google to request a reevaluation.

You can do this via the Contact Us page (http://goo.gl/6wypv). Click the Email Us link at the bottom of the page. Complete the provided form, including a detailed description of the issue and resolution. If there was a problem and it's been corrected, then it's best to be clear and state both the history and the corrective actions you took.

In the US, you can also call 1-866-2Google (9 AM to 8 PM EST). Have your AdWords customer number ready (you can find it on the top toolbar when logged into AdWords).

If you've requested that Google re-evaluate improperly-penalized landing pages, keep an eye on your server logs for traffic from adsbot-google to know when they actually revisit the page again. Of course, there is no way of knowing if they're coming to review your pages because of your request, but if you don't see visits from this crawler, it's a clear indication that progress is not occurring. Note that landing page scans are normally done infrequently; it can be days or weeks under normal circumstances before pages are checked or rechecked. Ultimately, if the bots rescan your page and the penalty is not lifted, it will be necessary for a human Google reviewer to override the work of the algorithm. This may require a second contact using one of the methods provided above.

Your AdWords Account Sucks

If business issues or landing page issues aren't the cause of your poor quality scores—and hopefully they aren't—the problem could simply be that your keyword selection, account structure, ad copy, and other AdWords attributions and options have been delivering what Google considers poor click-through-rates. In other words, you're earning your poor quality scores.

Understanding and accepting the fact that your quality score problems are the result of low CTRs (and poor AdWords relevance) is the first step toward improving them. Resolving the underlying issues will likely take a lot of work and a lot of changes. You're going to have to figure out exactly what's wrong, and then take action to correct it.

The worse shape your account is in, the more dramatically you should cut it back before building it up. All keywords not earning at least a 7 should be paused (or deleted if, upon reflection, they don't belong in the account). Re-expansion should happen slowly and follow the principles shared in *Chapter Eight: The Simple Path to Good Quality Scores.*

It's going to take time and effort. The management or clients you report to will have to understand and accept that it could take weeks or months, depending on the size of your account, to get back to anywhere near the number of keywords, revenue volume, or other metrics that existed before the rehab began. Account quality will rise, ROI will rise, and—if thoughtfully done—total revenue and profitability will both exceed past levels. But it will take time and effort.

But before you start that process, if the account is really in bad shape, you have a big decision to make: do you need to create a new AdWords account and, in effect, start over?

Starting Over with a New AdWords Account

When an AdWords account is filled with poor quality score keywords for a long enough time, AdWords eventually gets the idea that you're a lousy advertiser and probably always will be. At that point, the keyword or ad copy isn't the problem—it's the account history.

We've seen brand keywords with click-through rates over 20% that earn quality scores of 4 or 5. This suggests that the historical CTR of the account was so low for so long that no keywords in the account can ever earn a decent quality score again. Even if everything about a given keyword and its clicks are perfect, its quality score would still be low or very low.

When an AdWords account is in that state, most or all keywords will get low quality scores, impression counts will be low and may dwindle, and you'll overpay for whatever clicks remain. It's probably time to start over.

There are at least two circumstances when starting over might be a good idea:

1. **Bad Performance History**. When an account has performed extremely poorly for a long period of time (over a year), the impact of the lifetime CTR (and any other related metrics that may be considered) is so great that even "perfect" new keywords and management practices will result in low quality scores.

    Qsually when this happens, the account has been around a while, and either nobody was paying much attention to it or the people who did manage it are long gone. The account generally has a lot of problems: tons of broad match, huge ad groups, bad (if not toxic) landing pages, and terrible CTRs and quality scores. It's likely been in that state for one to three years or longer.

    Efforts to improve or rebuild the account have met with very little success. New keywords, narrow ad groups, relevant landing pages, and careful attention earn quality scores in the 2–5 range, even after they've had days or weeks to burn in. In the worst cases, even brand keywords getting double-digit CTRs earn quality scores below 6.

2. **Historic Penalties**. When an account has been penalized because of business model issues, site policy issues, landing page issues, or similar problems, even after those issues have been fully and completely resolved, the account may still never get out of penalty mode.

    Note that Google may or may not acknowledge account penalties. Attempting to communicate with them is important; acknowledge past problems and misbehavior and provide assurance that everything has been cleaned and now conforms to the rules and recommendations. But often, the results or reactions aren't clear or definitive. At some point, it's better just to give up and start over.

In this case, however, be aware that a) there may be a "flag" on the domain and a new account may not solve the problem; and b) if any of the prohibited activity is still going on, Google will likely find it and penalize you again. In other words, you have to deserve this second chance, and even then you may still need to contact Google (i.e., beg) to get it.

Unfortunately, it's their game, their rules. There is no third-party arbitration panel to go to for an appeal. You must please the Google gods, or sneak around them.

Starting over with a new AdWords account is not a decision to make lightly or an action to take impulsively. It's a drastic measure that takes a lot of time and energy, and if not done for the right reasons and in the right way, it won't have the desired effect.

WHEN REHAB IS BETTER THAN RESTART

If your account isn't terminal, but rather just a mixture of mediocre scores with a few really poor ones, don't create a new account. The presence of any great quality scores (8–10) or a reasonable percentage of good ones (7) strongly suggest that a restart isn't necessary and you should rehabilitate the account instead.

See the section titled Your AdWords Account Sucks earlier in this chapter, and chapters 8, 9, and 11 for more information on account rehab.

Note that the official Google AdWords Help Forum (http://goo.gl/7thRC) is a good place to get all kinds of questions answered, particularly if you have what seems like an incurable account. Assuming you've followed all the recommendations in this book, you can post a question about your situation and AdWords employees (and other experts) can offer advice and perhaps get you some help from inside Google to clear the curse off your account.

HOW TO RESTART

If you decide to restart in a new account, maximize your success by reading and following the suggestions in *Chapter Eight: The Simple Path to Good Quality Score*, which details the goals and best practices you'll want to keep in mind. Move slowly and deliberately through the process of creating and expanding your new account, or else risk creating another account full of poor quality scores.

The point of building a new account is to demonstrate that you deserve—and know how to earn—good quality scores. This means building up a great account quality score right from the start and excellent quality scores on initial keywords. Then, *slowly* add new keywords and prove that you can earn good or great quality scores on them too.

The philosophy of the new account should be "winners only." There's a reason you're going through this exercise. It may be that there was a terrible historical quality score, or currently underserved penalties associated with the account, but it was likely also due in part to having too many low relevance, low CTR, and low quality score keywords in the account. It's also likely that all the ad groups and keywords in the old account weren't thoughtfully optimized; the work necessary to figure out the correct keywords, match types, negatives, and ad copy wasn't done. If tougher requirements and better procedures aren't followed in the new account, there is no reason to believe it will earn better quality scores.

With that in mind, here's a four-step plan for effectively creating your new account:

1. Avoid duplicate accounts trouble.
2. Start with winners.
3. Expand slowly.
4. Losers are not allowed.

Avoid Duplicate Accounts Trouble

Before you can begin the transition to a new AdWords account, you have to create it. There are restrictions on an advertiser using more than one account for a single business, and Google has banned advertisers for violating them, so read this section carefully and, if possible, talk to your Google rep before and during the transition process.

Here's what Google says about having multiple AdWords accounts:

> *Can I have multiple AdWords accounts?*
>
> *No. In order to preserve the quality and diversity of ads running on Google, individuals advertising for themselves or for their own businesses may only have a single AdWords account unless explicitly advised otherwise by Google.*
>
> *This means that we don't allow advertisers or affiliates to have any of the following:*
>
> - *Ads across multiple accounts for the same or similar businesses*
> - *Ads across multiple accounts triggered by the same or similar keywords*
>
> *Only client managers (such as third parties or search engine marketers) who use a My Client Center can have multiple AdWords accounts. All associated accounts must be linked to the manager's My Client Center account.*
>
> Source: http://goo.gl/jtpU0

This seems to state clearly that you cannot have two AdWords accounts for the same company. But it's not that simple. There is a legitimate way to have multiple accounts:

1. Create the new account using the same name, address, and credit card as the existing account.

2. Associate each of your accounts with a single MCC (MyClientCenter) as described above. This lets Google know that you're not secretly trying to run multiple ads for the same site from different accounts—a bannable offense known as "double-serving."

3. Never run the same keywords in more than one account at the same time. Doing so would be an attempt at double-serving and will lead to trouble.

4. Talk to your Google rep (if you have one) and get permission (or acknowledgement) for your plan to use more than one account (even temporarily). Google regularly grants permission for advertisers (usually large ones) to use multiple accounts on a permanent basis. Make clear to them your adherence to steps 1 through 3.

In the AdWords Help Forum, a Google staffer answered a question about using two AdWords accounts within a single company to separate low and high quality score keywords:

> *I think your overall strategy is a pretty good one—keeping the lower quality keywords separate from your high performing keywords—very smart. And, if you put those two accounts in an MCC and link them, it shouldn't be a problem as long as there is no keyword overlap across the two accounts.*
>
> Source: http://goo.gl/M5p5d

A simple strategy to avoid any issue, of course, is simply to cancel or pause all the campaigns in your old AdWords account before starting work on the new one. That's a good idea if the old one was really horrible, assuming you can afford a temporary drop in traffic.

Sometimes that's an easy decision because the old account is in such bad shape it's not driving any traffic, but if it *is* driving traffic that's necessary to the business, then a slow transition is necessary. To do this properly and effectively, set up the new account following the guidelines above, and be very careful to pause or delete each keyword in the old account when you begin to run a version of it in the new one.

Start with Winners

Begin the new account with only your very best keywords—ideally just a few dozen at most. The very best way to start is with your brand keywords or other terms that had very high CTRs and excellent quality scores in your old account. If the old account had no keywords with good quality scores due to an account penalty of some kind, then definitely start with only core brand terms. If you don't have any brand terms, then begin with a small number of very specific "long tail" keywords for which you have an excellent message and offer and will likely be able to earn good or very good click-through rates.

After identifying the dozen or three keywords you want to start with (less is better), create small ad groups, write great targeted copy, geo-target narrowly if appropriate, and bid into positions 5 or higher (preferably 2 to 4), at least for the first week or so. Don't be too alarmed by very low quality scores in the initial days.

Note that if the display URL in the new account is the same as that used in the old account, the past performance of ads to that display URL is taken into account and can hurt your initial quality score. Similarly, if you use the exact same pairs of keywords and text ad copy as was used in the old account, according to Google the historical performance from the old account will be considered (more on this later).

During the first week or two, this first batch of keywords will gather clicks and their quality scores should rise and stabilize, hopefully at 7 or higher. It may take several days—up to two weeks—before scores stabilize and reach these levels. Don't add any more keywords before this happens.

If you have a known brand (one that people go to Google and search on with some regularity), it's not unusual to see double-digit click-through rates and quality scores of 10. That's why brand keywords are a great way to start off a new AdWords account.

After your initial batch of keywords has hit or exceeded quality scores of 7 and remained at that level for at least a few days, you can begin thinking about expanding the new account and adding more ad groups and keywords.

But it would be better if you didn't. The best way to build up a great historical CTR in a new account is leave only your initial small group of very high-CTR keywords running for weeks or even months. This process of establishing a good initial historical CTR for the account is sometimes called "burning in" an account. At a minimum, your first and best keywords should be allowed to run for about two weeks, or a few thousand impressions, to clearly demonstrate stability and success in quality score before starting expansion.

The longer the history of high initial quality scores you can create, the better the residual effects will be when you start expanding. As described earlier, the calculation of quality score moves from general to specific over time. Initially, each set of new keywords added to the account may place a heavier than normal emphasis on the account-level CTR until they garner significant impression and CTR histories of their own. Given the goal of the new account, it's helpful for your account-level metrics to be as strong as possible.

It's impossible to quantify the specific benefit of a long burn-in period, and for most advertisers, more than a few weeks probably isn't practical anyway. Think of each week after the initial two as giving your account a little bit of a stronger backbone, but when you've got to expand the account, then begin expanding the account.

Expand Slowly

With your CTR and quality score base established, you're ready to expand the account. Expansion should take place in phases; at each stage, add another set of keywords and ad groups, manage and optimize them to achieve good or great quality scores, and then allow those scores to prove their stability and add to your historical CTR before moving on to the next set of keywords.

Expansion should be managed based on the number of impressions generated by each group of keywords. If your initial set of keywords were getting 25,000 impressions per week, then the first expansion set should include only keywords expected to get 50,000 to 75,000 impressions per week. In other words, only add enough keywords to double or triple your impression count. This prevents the new keywords from overwhelming the history built up by the original keywords.

Note that as you add keywords, their initial quality scores are calculated using all the criteria described in Chapter Five and are influenced by your old account as mentioned above (via display URL and keyword + ad copy if identical). The influence of the historical CTR of the new account will be considered.

When you advertise on keywords you haven't advertised on before, Google considers the results other advertisers have had with that keyword. So if you see a low initial quality score, that probably means that others have had a hard time doing well (quality score–wise) with that keyword. If it doesn't rise relatively quickly, it may not be a good keyword to use in your new account.

Once the expansion keywords have stabilized and earned (or been optimized to earn) good quality scores, the account is ready for another expansion. Continue to expand only at the rate of two or three times the most recent average impression volume.

Losers Not Allowed

As you expand your new account, keep an eye on average CTRs and the distribution of quality scores. Don't allow poorly performing keywords or low quality scores to remain active. Keep high standards in your new account—or it will turn into your old account.

One important way to protect your new account is to be very cautious before adding any of the worst-performing keywords from the old account. If you don't understand why they were doing poorly (especially if not all of your keywords were scoring that low), then consider giving up on them.

If you must try to rehabilitate, add them to a special "quarantined" campaign and put them on a very short leash. If they can't perform in the new environment, give up quickly.

Moving Quality Scores

According to Google, quality score history is "stored" with keywords, ads, and target URLs, and if any of these items (or more importantly, several of them at once) move from one AdWords account to another, their quality score–related history will move with them. It's not exactly that quality score itself moves with the keyword—quality score is calculated in real time in the new account just like it was in the old one–but some of the "contributing scores" will be (according to Google) transferred.

Unless you're able to move your website to a new domain at the same time you create the new AdWords account, the continued use of the same root domain in your target URLs will result in transference of some of the old "bad history" to the new account. But in calculating quality scores, these transferring factors will be considered alongside the new factors like account CTR history.

For keywords that were performing well, it's a good idea to move them and their associated ad copy and target URLs over exactly, and also use the same landing page (or at least one that won't be rated Poor). Don't expect your old quality score to transfer immediately, though; Google says that even when moving keywords to a new ad group in the same account, it can take weeks for all the new factors to be considered and the quality score to stabilize. It's probably best to think of this not as any guarantee or entitlement, but as a mere advantage: history will be on your side, but in reality, you'll still have to earn each keyword's quality score.

For keywords that had poor performance and quality scores in the old account (the reason you're moving to a new account), this suggests you'll want to make as many changes as possible. Organize into ad groups differently, write new ad copy, use new target URLs, and of course make sure the landing pages won't be rated Poor.

Working in a new account sheds some but not all of your problem history. It can give you a chance to resurrect AdWords as a successful platform, but you'll have to deliver improved performance or the new account will be a lot of wasted effort.

Chapter Summary

When faced with the responsibility for an account full of poor or terrible quality scores, you've got your work cut out for you. Not only with Google, but in most cases also with your managers or clients who must understand and accept that the situation is:

- **Serious**. The performance of the account is severely compromised in term of both excess cost and diminished volume, and it will remain so until corrected.

- **Difficult**. The decisions, work, cost, and time required to fix a broken account are hard to bear. It could take six months to do the work properly—assuming it can be done at all. During that time, traffic and revenue will severely diminish.

- **Required**. The only alternative is to accept the status quo. Throwing money at the problem will help, but only a little, and perhaps not permanently. It's time to pay the piper.

Of course, the truth is that most accounts that are full of terrible quality scores are that way for a very good reason. It's Google's game and they make the rules. Through intention or ignorance, someone (or a group of someones) did something wrong. They may have gotten away with violating some of these rules for a while, but over time, most get caught and punished. If that happens to you, you may or may not get a second chance. If you do, take it seriously and use it wisely.

Chapter Eleven:
Everyday Quality Score Management

If your account isn't dominated by very low quality scores and doesn't suffer from any account-wide penalties or problems, then your path to improving quality scores will take place one keyword at a time.

This chapter will walk you through the methodical process of finding and eliminating issues that can drag down the quality score of any keyword. Our methods are simply the everyday blocking and tackling of good paid search management. We'll help you rule out issues that are harmful to quality score and implement a series of best practices that generally drive quality score upward.

You'll also learn about some techniques (like query mining) and special situations (like keywords that are too narrowly targeted) that will help you to become a certified quality score master. In the end, we'll help you work to accept that not all quality scores can be raised, and we'll talk about why, when, and how to give up the quest and simply turn away from, or turn off, a keyword that's stuck with a low quality score.

What to Expect

Before sitting down to make changes to your keywords in an effort to improve their quality scores, you should have realistic expectations about the way your efforts can actually impact keyword quality scores.

If your keywords aren't suffering from low quality scores due to one of the specific issues discussed in *Chapter Ten: Dealing with Disaster*, then there will rarely be a clear connection between a change you make and a resulting quality score change. As we've discussed in prior chapters, quality scores are impacted by a range of factors and variables, and there's a lot we still don't know about the rules or calculation of quality score.

This means that a portion of your quality score management efforts have to be faith-based. You must take actions that you know to be right—that will create a better-structured, more efficient, and theoretically more pleasing-to-the-customer campaign—even without quick or obvious results. You have to watch for results, scrutinize them, think carefully about your actions and potential actions, and then move forward, even if those results don't tell you anything or temporarily suggest moving backward.

Expect a lot of detective work and experimentation. Clear and decisive wins will occur along the way, but often, the bulk of your results will simply be broad slow movement in the right direction.

When Quality Score Won't Improve

Keep in mind that you won't be able to improve the quality score of every keyword. There are several reasons why that little number just may not budge:

1. **The wrong people are seeing your ads**. Some keywords attract users with such a diverse set of desires that earning the kind of CTR required for a good quality score is effectively impossible.

2. **The people seeing the ads don't find your ads compelling**. Other keywords attract people who you might want to visit your site but who just aren't interested in your offers. So unless the offers change, or at least the ad copy, the scores will remain the same.

3. **A site, landing page, business model, or industry penalty is in effect**. The problem could be something beyond your click-through rates.

4. **Google is getting it wrong**. AdWords manages millions upon millions of keywords in a very complex environment. Their system and algorithms aren't flawless. You will encounter results that make no sense—keywords with very high CTRs and low quality scores, for example.

The majority of this chapter describes strategies and tactics to improve quality scores in these situations. But in case that doesn't work, near the end of the chapter we'll review some rules of thumb to help you decide when it makes more sense to hit the pause button and give up on a particular keyword.

Visible Quality Scores Updates

Another challenge you face when working to improve quality score is that there's no clear way to know when a particular keywords score has been recalculated or updated. Your most recent changes may have had no effect, or they may have had a profound effect but you can't tell because the score hasn't been updated yet.

Quality Score updates are pushed forward into your account based on the volume of impressions and clicks the keyword receives. This means some of the keywords in an ad group may have been updated today, and others may have not been updated for a week or more. It's likely—but entirely unproven—that keywords getting even a few dozen impressions per week have their visual quality scores updated every few days or at least once per week. With new keywords, it's common to see scores move every day or two from the time they're first created until they "settle in," so it doesn't seem unreasonable to assume a similar pace for existing keyword updates.

It's safe to assume that quality scores update every few days at worst for active keywords, new keywords, when changing match types, or when testing new text ad copy.

Other issues, such as historical CTR problems or business model penalties, may take much longer to resolve—sometimes weeks or months. Landing page issues can also take weeks in some cases. Patience is a required tool in your quality score repair toolbox.

Prioritizing Your Work

So where should you start? In accounts with tens or hundreds of thousands of keywords, there is always vastly more to do than time allows. What's the best way to decode which keywords to work on first?

There are at least three ways you might want to prioritize your time:

- **Follow the Money**. Sort keywords in descending order of cost or revenue and manicure the tops of those lists first. Given the impact volume has on quality score, you may also want to sort by impression count. How far you're able to work down these lists depends, of course, on resources. Fortunately, the "head" of these lists is usually narrow, with only a few dozen or a few hundred keywords with substantial costs, revenues, or impressions. The tail starts at a small fraction of the head's volume, so when the numbers get small, you can move on without too much guilt.

- **Strategic Importance**. A secondary but still important priority is to work on keywords or ad groups that are of strategic importance to current business results or future business goals. When these kinds of strategic keywords are earning poor quality scores, they may have low costs, revenues, and impressions, so they won't pop onto your regularly priority lists. Spending time on these may be a prerequisite to them making your top performer lists, so of course you should spend time optimizing them.

- **Worst First**. Keywords with low quality scores probably have the greatest chance for improvement and will harm your account until they are fixed or removed. Spending time fixing or choosing to pause keywords with quality scores below 5 and then seeing if you can improve those with 5s or 6s is certainly a logical way to start.

Whichever method you choose, it's a good idea to have some strategy to guide the use of your time. This not only ensures that you're spending your time effectively, but it also makes it easier to track your work and results over days or weeks.

The Top Ten Ways to

Improve the Quality Score of Any Keyword

Based on what you've learned about the factors that influence quality score, it's a fairly straightforward exercise to create a task list to identify and remove quality score barriers and promote quality score boosters.

Your goal is simple: create keywords that are free of quality score penalties (at the account or keyword level) and earn good or great click-through rates. This requires keywords that attract interested people to your ads, and ads that deliver compelling and persuasive ad copy. All the principles of good quality score management described in *Chapter Eight: The Simple Path to Good Quality Scores* will apply.

The nine-step plan below tackles the issues that can impact the quality score of any keyword in order from most to least impactful. Walking through these steps will help you to ensure that every keyword you work on is set up for the best possible quality score.

Step 1: Rule out Landing Page Penalties

Check for a keyword-specific landing page problem by looking in AdWords at the pop-up window offered in the Status column. If the landing page is rated "Poor," then your first order of business is to correct any potential issues that may be causing this status. You'll never earn a good quality score until this is resolved. See *Chapter 10: Dealing With Disaster* for more information on what makes a "Poor" landing page.

Step 2: Rule out Poor Relevance

Check for poor relevance by looking in AdWords at the pop-up window offered in the Status column. If relevance is rated as "Poor," then you'll either have to make dramatic changes to improve relevance or consider pausing or deleting the keyword. It's extremely difficult to earn good quality scores with poor relevance.

Poor relevance is a reflection of particularly poor CTR, either in general, in specific geo-target markets, or as related to factors Google won't clearly reveal. In any case, it's a clear indication that the keyword is attracting queries that are inappropriate or not well served by the ads being displayed. The corrective action is generally to follow the steps in the balance of this list, but the fact that relevance has been flagged means you'll really have to move the needle to "save" this keyword. See *Chapter Five: How Quality Score Is Calculated* for more information on relevance.

STEP 3: RULE OUT SLOW PAGE LOAD TIMES

Check page load time in AdWords in the pop-up window offered in the Status column. Load time is considered slow if it takes three or more seconds than your regional average to load the HTML portion of your page from a fast connection within the United States. Performance is measured over time, so don't worry about one bad day or a little down time. But if your page is rated "Poor," then you'll have to speed it up, perhaps by following the suggestions AdWords provides here: http://goo.gl/nuzGd

STEP 4: DECIDE IF THE KEYWORD IS WORTH FIXING

If one of the above three problems isn't blocking a good quality score, then it's going to take some effort to figure out and correct the real problem. Before beginning this work, take a few moments to consider whether or not the keyword is worth the effort. Is it relevant to you and your business? It is a wise keyword to have in your account? Would you be surprised if it's an unprofitable participant? Is it going to drive enough volume to justify the time and effort it's going to take to try to improve the quality score? If the keyword doesn't belong or isn't likely to succeed, then you're probably better off pausing or deleting it than spending a lot of time and effort trying in vain to improve its quality score. One of the main purposes of quality score is to get advertisers to bid only on keywords that are likely to satisfy searchers and earn relevant clicks. Turning off keywords is a natural and healthy part of the paid search management process.

STEP 5: REVIEW AND REACT TO THE SEARCH QUERIES

For broad and phrase match keywords that don't have good or great quality scores, you should review the search query report and actively create new keywords based on the most effective, interesting, and relevant queries so that each term can earn its own, hopefully higher, quality score.

This effort won't improve the quality score of the current keyword; to do that you'll have to continue working through our list. But it is a critical step toward maximizing the quality score and results of your account.

This step is necessary because quality score is only calculated when the search query is identical to the keyword. When the keyword is matched to any other query, quality score is calculated based on how the keyword performed for matching queries. So queries resulting from broad or phrase matches are borrowing quality score—which may not be to your advantage, especially when the quality score is low. By creating an independent keyword, the term will earn its own quality score. Of course, to maximize that score you'll want to place the new keyword in an ad group with highly targeted and relevant ad copy, which may mean creating a new ad group and writing new ad copy.

More information on this process is provided in the discussion on query mining found later in this chapter.

STEP 6: CREATE SMALLER AD GROUPS

Look at all the keywords in the same ad group as the keyword you're working on, and then look at the current set of text ads for that ad group. Can you think of a way to break the keywords into two or more ad groups so that your ad copy can be more directly responsive to the unique concepts represented by the keywords?

If so, then do it. Break the keywords down into smaller ad groups and write tailored and targeted ad copy for two or more text ads in each group.

Step 7: Write Better Ad Copy

If a keyword is well targeted in terms of driving queries to appropriate text ads, then your best shot at improving quality score is to significantly improve click-through rate. And the best way to do that is almost always via better ad copy.

Before starting to write new copy, look for significant CTR differences between your best and worst performing ads within a single ad group, and at the difference between average CTRs for different ad groups within a single campaign. Cull out the losers—anything with a CTR lower than its peers by 30% to 50% or more (based on a statistically significant sample).

It's also worth looking at the CTR differences between keywords within the ad group. If you compare the CTRs of different keywords in the same ad group with different quality scores (the CTRs of the 5s vs. the CTRs of the 7s, for example), you will often see the localized relationship between CTR and quality score. The keywords that underperform in terms of CTR are doing so for some reason—most likely because they're attracting the wrong queries or are matched with ineffective ad copy.

When everything is targeted properly and known poor performers have been eliminated, it's time to start writing and testing new ad copy. Leave the best-performing existing ad running, and introduce one or two new creative ads into the ad group. Give them sufficient time to prove themselves or fail (usually a few hundred impressions or a few dozen clicks), but once you have significant data, kill the losers and let the winners ride (or better yet, be tested against another new crop). Ad copy must communicate, differentiate, and persuade. If it can't do that, it can't earn the clicks and the quality scores.

Step 8: Try a Higher Average Position

Position isn't supposed to matter for quality score. But Google's ability to compensate for the positional influence on CTR is far from perfect. Keywords that spend most of their time low on the page (positions 6–8) may benefit from a few weeks (or a few hundreds clicks) in the middle (positions 3–5) or at the top. Of course, without raising quality score, the only way to raise positions is to bid higher, so this can be an expensive test. But if you believe the keyword has potential and the ad copy is strong, and none of the above steps resolve the issue, then buying your way to the middle (or the top) and seeing if the keyword performs or is evaluated differently there might be worth considering.

STEP 9: CONSIDER A DIFFERENT DISPLAY URL

The historic click-through rate of the display URL in the ads associated with any keyword has a small impact on that keyword's quality score. It's highly unlikely to be a driving factor in any particularly poor scores, but if you're trying to eliminate all potential issues or are looking for every advantage possible on a keyword, then insert a display URL that has only been used with keywords that have earned good or great quality scores in the past.

STEP 10: STOP RUNNING ADS IN POORLY PERFORMING GEOGRAPHIES

The visible quality score of any keyword in your account is based on CTR measures across all geographies where ads are displayed, even if the keyword is targeted at different geographies in different campaigns. If your keywords get low click-through rates in specific geographic areas, you can boost the keyword's visible quality score throughout your account by pausing it in those poorly performing regions.

It is important to note, however, that due to differences between visible quality score and quality score for ad rank and CPC, pausing keywords in poorly performing regions will have little or no impact on your costs or positions, even in regions with strong performance. This tactic is primarily an effort to get your visible quality score to more accurately reflect the quality score the keywords are earning in those areas where you clicks are coming from. It may, however, have a positive effect on the lifetime click-through rate of your account and the CTR of the display URLs associated with your text ads.

There are two ways to determine the geographies where ads should not be run. One is to separate geographic campaigns by geography and then pause keywords in any regions with low CTRs relative to the other regions. The second is to review your conversion rates by geography and exclude regions where the conversion rates are particularly low. This method may or may not remove those geographies where CTR is low, but it's an easier process than having to create many geo-targeted campaigns for each of your keywords.

LAST THOUGHTS ON THE TEN-STEP PLAN

Based on the earlier chapters of this book, the steps in this plan probably weren't much of a surprise. Hopefully this simple sequence makes sense based on what you've learned. Asking these questions about a keyword and thoughtfully resolving (or at least working to improve on) any imperfections you find in the answers should eliminate the vast majority of issues that cause low CTR and therefore low quality scores.

Keyword Expansion and Query Mining

Quality score is reported at the keyword level, but it's a mistake to think about it as a keyword-level attribute. Quality score reflects the relationship between keywords, search queries, ad copy, and the searcher. So another way to manage quality score is to manage this relationship.

When you change the keywords in your account, either by adding new variations of existing keywords or new keywords based on search queries that were matched to existing keywords, you change the dynamics by which quality score was being measured. Modifying the keyword themselves is itself a way to manage quality score. Expanding your use of negative keywords can also improve CTR and quality score. (You may have heard the rumor that negative keywords cannot help quality score, which is based on the fact that visible quality score only considers queries identical to the keyword. But the historical CTR of the account and other measures as used by quality score for ad rank and CPC do benefit from the increased click-through rate produced by proper use of negative keywords.)

SEARCH QUERY REPORTS

In AdWords and in third-party tools, you can review the search queries that Google has matched to your keywords. This presents a huge opportunity to improve and impact quality score. When reviewing the search queries being matched to broad match and phrase match keywords, you will likely be inspired to:

- Add negative keywords

- Add new phrase and exact match keywords

- Create new ad groups

- Write new ad copy

Keyword	Search Query
+vitamins For +parrots	vitamin pills 4 parrots
Multi +vitamins For +parrots	multyvitamins for parrots sugar free
+parrots +supplements	chewable supplements for small parrots
+parrot +supplements	buy rf-1 parrot supplement
+parrot +supplements	cpn parrot supplements
+parrot +supplements	standard process parrot supplements
birdbrain +supplement For +parrot	birdbrain supplement for parrot heart
birdbrain +supplement For +parrot	physical locations in colorado for birdbrain parrot supplements
Holistic +supplements For +parrots	supplement for muscles and bones for parrots holistic
Bladder +supplements For +parrots	supplements for parrots with leaky bladders
+supplements For +parrots	proprietary glucosamine supplements for parrots
+chick +supplements	best supplements for chick
+parrot +car +sick	tips to help a car sick parrot
parrot Motion Sickness	parrots motion sickness
parrot Motion Sickness	car sick parrots
+allergy +pet +pet +food	pet food allergies in parrots
All +birdbrain +pet +food Store	all birdbrain petfood
birdbrain Flea	natiual fleas snd ticks
birdbrain Flea	birdbrain tick & flee guard
birdbrain Flea	birdbrain tick yard
Flea Control birdbrain	flea control candles
Flea Control birdbrain	birdbrain products to repel fleas and ticks
Flea Control birdbrain	this birdbrain product really gets rid of fleas
birdbrain Flea And Tick	best herbel flee and tick for cockatoos
Outdoor birdbrain Flea Control	birdbrain spray for fleas in yard

This process is called query mining. Each resulting change can improve click-through rates, impression share, and quality score. Query mining improves your PPC account in two specific ways relative to quality score:

1) **Better focus**. Every new negative keyword reduces wasted impressions, and every new exact or phrase match keyword can increase the volume of targeted impressions. This process of narrowing or repositioning your funnel–aiming at a more appropriate set of people with your ads–sets the stage for higher and higher click-through rates.

2) **More Precision**. Since visible quality score is only calculated when a search query is identical to a keyword, you can't see the visible quality score associated with the majority of search queries that are matched to keywords in your account. Every time you create a new keyword based on a search query that was formerly matched to another keyword, you make it possible for that keyword to earn its own visible quality score and you create the option to move that keyword into a new ad group to match it with the most targeted and compelling ad copy possible.

Suppose you bid on the broad match keyword "dog food" and it earns a visible quality score of 5. That quality score is based on how the keyword performs when the query is "dog food." If the CTR is higher when that keyword is matched to a query like "organic dog food store in Boston," then the quality score for ad rank and quality score for CPC will be better—but you won't know it because you never get to see those versions of quality score.

But suppose you notice that the search query "organic dog food store in Boston" has a high number of conversions, so you create a new keyword based on that query:

♦ dog food store (broad match)

♦ "dog food store in Boston" (phrase match)

♦ [organic dog food store in Boston] (exact match)

Assuming performance remains consistent, when visible quality score stabilizes for these new keywords, it will reflect the higher CTR and be better than the quality score for "dog food." Assuming all other variables are constant—the same ad copy, visible URL, etc.—there will be no difference in the quality scores for ad rank or CPC . Instead, what you accomplished by creating a separate keyword was visibility for the quality score based on certain queries.

If you take the time to move the new keyword into a new or different ad group and write ad copy to mention "store" and even "Boston," then both CTR and quality score are likely to move even higher. The point is that all queries not identical to the keywords they match are at risk of never realizing their quality score potential.

The other benefit you'd realize in this example is that these new keywords would likely become eligible for a different set of search queries than the original keyword because of their words, match types, and performance. If you think of queries as existing in a cloud around the keyword (as discussed earlier in regard to the determination of eligibility), adding a new keyword is like adding a new magnet off in a slightly different position in the cloud. Naturally, it's going to do a better job of attracting search queries near its location. This should lead to increased impression volume, impression share, and clicks from highly relevant (and therefore hopefully highly converting) search queries near that new keyword. Of course, over time you can watch the search query report for the new keywords and refine the process further with additional query mining.

The process of query mining is straightforward. Review the search queries that have been clicked for each of your broad and phrase matched keywords (or at least your most clicked keywords) and then:

1. Add a new negative keyword to the ad group or campaign, using all or part of the query, for any queries or partial queries that are unrelated or poorly targeted.

2. Consider using modified broad match to require certain terms from multi-word broad match keywords by adding the + sign in front of them. This makes individual words "required" in any query matched to that broad match keyword, thereby greatly narrowing the range of queries that will be matched.

3. Add a new keyword with phrase or exact match type for any queries or partial queries that convert or seem particularly well focused or targeted.

4. Create these new keywords in a new ad group and write targeted copy if they would not be best served by the existing copy in the existing ad group.

5. Move existing keywords into new or different ad groups in order to better align them and their queries with targeted ad copy.

LAST THOUGHTS ON QUERY MINING

In *Chapter 8: The Simple Path to Good Quality Scores*, the first principle we suggested to earn great click-through rates and therefore high quality scores was to target only searchers likely to be interested in your offer. There is no better way to improve targeting in your account than via query mining. It uses search queries as the ultimate keyword research tool, allows you to eliminate waste by avoiding non-targeted searchers, improves the precision of your quality score reporting, and makes it much easier to align the question implicit in every search query with compelling answers delivered via your ad copy. Query mining is a process that can't help but improve quality scores and economic results by improving nearly every aspect of your paid search account.

Fracturing Keywords for Quality Score Clues

While creating new keywords based on search queries can improve focus and precision in your quality score management and reporting, having multiple instances of the same keyword in different ad groups or campaigns can provide a different kind of utility.

As you'll recall from *Chapter Four: Which Quality Score*, visible quality score for any keyword aggregates the performance of all versions of a keyword within your account. If the keyword "Elvis Costello Tickets" is in your account 30 different times—in broad, phrase, and exact match formats in ten different geo-targeted campaigns, for example—then every one of them will always have the same visible quality score.

But the performance metrics reported for each keyword instance can be very informative and beneficial. You may see that the exact match version has a 16% CTR, while the broad match version has only a 1.6% CTR, driving you to review the broad match search query report and query mine like crazy. You may see that the conversion rate in Florida is only 40% of what it is in California and rewrite your ad copy or even set your bids accordingly.

In both of these cases, splitting a single keywords into multiple versions enables you to see data that impacts quality score for ad rank and quality score for CPC but does not affect visible quality score. This includes the performance of search queries that are not identical to the keyword, and performances in specific geographies. Both are considered as part of the relevance component of quality score as explained in *Chapter Five: How Quality Score Is Calculated.* They matter, but they're never reported in any visible way in the current implementation of quality score.

In the case of geo-specific performance, you should monitor results and opt out of advertising in any particularly poorly performing areas. The only way to do this is to create separate campaigns with different regional geo-targeting. AdWords doesn't offer this kind of reporting granularity in campaigns targeted to a single national geography. Even third-party analytics and paid search platforms that report on the geography of each click don't enable you to calculate geo-specific CTR because geo-specific impression data isn't available.

Using campaigns that are regionally geo-targeted (by state, for example) makes it easy to see state-vs.-state CTR differences, although you'll need significant impression and CTR volumes in each geography for these metrics to be mathematically significant and therefore useful. In order to get meaningful volumes, you may have to use larger regions for each campaign than you may like.

If you do break existing campaigns into multiple geo-targeted versions, in addition to providing a more refined level of reporting, geo-targeting campaigns at the state level causes AdWords to display the name of the searcher's state or region beneath the ad. This extra line has been reported to increase CTR by many advertisers. And higher CTR, as you may know, leads to higher quality scores!

When Keywords Are Too Targeted

Here comes a contradiction. Throughout this book, we've advised caution when bidding on broad concept keywords and topics and recommended instead that you try to find keywords that suggest specific intent. You may even have the idea that your keywords should be as narrow and specific and specialized as possible.

Broadly speaking, this is great advice. But it's possible to go too far, and as with many aspects of AdWords, there are exceptions to the rule. The problem isn't so much with the super-targeted keywords themselves, but rather with the way that Google decides quality scores in these cases. Ultra-specific, long-long-tail, hyper-focused keywords have two attributes that work against you in the game of quality score:

1. You may be the first advertisers in the history of AdWords ever to bid on that keyword.

2. They keyword may get a very low number of impressions and clicks because it's aimed at such an uber-narrow, and therefore small or infrequent, audience.

These attributes conspire to give Google very little data to work with when trying to predict how these keyword will perform, which makes it difficult for them to predict performance and therefore set a quality score for these keywords.

Suppose for example your company begins selling the world's first "red faux-leather buffalo-scented electric steering wheel cover," and you even manage to get your press release picked up by the online version of *Car and Driver Magazine*. Naturally, you would add a bunch of related keywords to a new campaign in your AdWords account: "buffalo-scented electric steering wheel cover" and [red faux-leather steering while cover] and a few dozen other combinations.

When AdWords first sees these keywords, they won't know what to make of them. They'll find no history in their databases of other advertisers setting click-through rate standards. They'll probably also see that in the history of the universe, there have been very few search queries that would have matched these keywords anyway. They're going to be suspicious.

Your new keywords will likely initially be assigned very low quality scores, almost certainly 5 or less. This will of course depend upon factors such as the account historical CTR and clues from your display URLs (if you don't assign a new one to the text ads you associate with these new keywords), but while more conventional new keywords in your account may jump right to 7, it's less likely in this case.

intelligent ppc bid management sofware   💬 Low search volume

You may even find that AdWords classifies the keywords as having "low search volume" and suspends them. This isn't as disastrous as it sounds:

> *"Low search volume" keywords are keywords associated with very little search traffic on Google properties. In which case, we suspend your keyword. This state is only temporary, and these keywords will be reactivated if we find that they could start delivering traffic.*
>
> *A keyword can have low search volume for a variety of reasons, including a lack of relevance to users' searches because of keyword obscurity, specificity, or a significant misspelling of the intended keyword. Keeping these keywords out of the ad auction helps AdWords serve ads more efficiently and reduces the volume of keywords on our system. Before stopping a keyword from joining the auction, our system evaluates the number of searches on a given keyword worldwide over the past twelve months. It takes very little search traffic for a keyword to be unsuspended, and for business practice reasons we don't disclose our keyword traffic thresholds. Our system checks and updates this status once per week.*

Source: http://goo.gl/4MrTZ

In other words, Google can't afford to have keywords in AdWords that will only match some small number of weekly searches. So to save their system work, and therefore allow it to perform well for the millions of other keywords that do match an active search query volume, they take them out of the game—but only until the search volume on those keywords builds

Showing ads right now?

> No   • This keyword has a low search volume and isn't showing any of your ads. If more users start searching for your keyword, your ad will begin to show. If you're interested in additional keyword ideas, try the Keyword Tool. Learn more about building an effective keyword list.

up to a sufficient level. So if you're buying a keyword and nobody (or nearly nobody) is searching for it, your job is to get people to search for it before you can try to be the answer to their searches. Put out a press release (that's how demand is generated, isn't it?), or hold a webinar, or write some articles on blogs, or otherwise make the terms you're promoting popular. As soon as people search, Google will happily run the auctions and display your ads and take your money.

When keywords are suspended due to low search volume, you can leave them active in your account, and there will be no negative effect of any kind. If and when search volume picks up, the keyword will reactivate. Your other option is to create different, less specific keywords to try to capture any related traffic that isn't as detailed as the keywords you had attempted. This can be tricky, as usually there is a keyword or phrase that defines the intent you were trying to capture.

Wave a White Flag

In *Chapter Nine: Quality Score Management*, we introduced the idea that keywords with quality scores below a certain threshold should be paused or deleted. We talked about the many ways you might think about the value and purpose of each keyword, suggested that sometimes keywords with poor quality scores are good for business, and tried to provide a framework for thinking about quality score management at the account level rather than at the keyword level. We also mentioned earlier in this chapter that some of those paused keywords should perhaps be put through the ten-step plan discussed above in an attempt to rehabilitate them and turn them back into productive assets.

With all of that in mind, and following the ten-step plan and discussion of query mining presented in this chapter, it's time to revisit the idea that pausing or deleting keywords is a viable and important quality score management technique.

There are keywords in your account that have poor quality scores and always will. Again, one way to think about poor quality scores is as a message from Google suggesting that maybe you're not the right advertiser for this keyword. Keywords that can't earn quality scores of at least 6 (some may argue for 5, others would push it all the way to 7) after taking all the steps outlined thus far should be paused or deleted *unless* they deliver great ROI or strategic benefit despite their poor quality scores.

There's no shame in turning off keywords. There is far more shame in running poorly performing keywords endlessly without consideration for their individual results or the effect they're having on the rest of the keywords in the account.

Go ahead, just pause them already.

Chapter Summary

There are two kinds of quality score management: crisis management as discussed in *Chapter 10: Dealing with Disaster* and everyday management as discussed in this chapter. When all the major issues are out of the way, everyday quality score management is primarily best-practice-based paid search management: pick good keywords, match them with relevant and persuasive ads, and send people to targeted landing pages.

Once a campaign is well constructed and intelligently appointed, it does make sense to execute a process of elimination against the known detractors when an individual keyword isn't earning the score you might wish.

Quality score doesn't measure the quality of a keyword. It measures the quality of your management of that keyword. Unfortunately, none of these efforts, or even all of them combined, can guarantee good or great quality scores. So part of the management job is to know when the only way to win is not to play. Luckily, in the vast majority of cases, following these recommendations will result in a great many good or great quality scores, and more importantly, in strong traffic volumes and (if your bids are reasonable) great results with a positive return on investment.

AfterWords

AdWords is a complex system in which advertisers spend millions of dollars in an effort to make many millions more. It's a zero-sum game with a finite number of searches and ad impressions. Anyone who chooses to advertise and put serious money into that effort should expect to have to work hard to understand the system, best their competition, and operate profitably.

AdWords is an amazing marketing and advertising platform. Compared to almost everything that came before it, it is elegant, efficient, transparent, manageable, and profitable. This is evidenced by the fact that nearly every other channel is evolving to be more like AdWords.

The AdWords system has an incredible natural advantages over most other marketing opportunities in that most of the population of the planet Earth regularly visit Google and specify their most immediate interest or need nearly exactly. Google has achieved its massive success by offering advertisers the chance to communicate with or offer a solution to these people.

Quality score is the not-so-secret ingredient that has allowed AdWords to grow and flourish. It creates a natural order among advertisers, delivers rationality to pricing, and forces bad actors out of the game.

Imperfections

Quality score is not without challenges or limitations for advertisers. The precise workings of the system have not been fully or clearly described, many of the metrics that drive the system are unavailable, and there is occasional unexpected behavior (either via errors or exceptions) for which which explanations and corrections have proven difficult to obtain.

Of course, it's unrealistic to expect perfection, even from Google. And Google doesn't operate AdWords exclusively in the best interests of advertisers; Google is running a business, after all. By and large, they have done an admirable job balancing the technical realities, development priorities, and their own business interets with the interests of searchers, and advertisers. AdWords has consistently and impressively improved over the years becoming more transparent and manageable, and there is every reason to expect continued improvements and evolution.

But as an advertiser you have to live in the here and now. You must play within the current rules and live with the restrictions of the current tools. The largest roadblock most advertisers or paid search managers face has been a lack of detailed technical and functional knowledge of the system. Google is partially responsible for not being more proactive with information and education, but the marketplace and user community hasn't done a particularly great job organizing, researching, testing, and sharing credible and practical information either. This book is hopefully a place for you to start while both sides work to level the information playing field.

With knowledge should come power, and we hope advertisers use this knowledge to request and even pressure Google to continue making our jobs easier with more data sharing and better tools.

Managing Quality

Even if the world isn't perfect, we believe that quality score is an overwhelmingly positive system for advertisers. In addition to its other functions, quality score presents advertisers with a technical roadmap and a moral compass that can be used to simplify the process of building and managing successful paid search accounts.

There is a lot of complexity to AdWords and to the application of quality score. We've tried to dig below the surface of as many quality score-related issues as possible throughout this book. But it's important to see the big picture too, and at that level the case for simplicity is compelling.

- Users have questions that they express via search queries.

- Advertisers who wish to answer those questions must earn the right by properly architecting and managing their campaigns.

- Quality score measures success by tracking click-through rate from many angles, and then rewards success or penalizes your lack thereof.

Your job managing paid search is to figure out which questions are in your economic interest to try to answer, and then to be one of the most effective advertisers on the planet at answering those questions. If you can do that, quality score and everything else will work out fine.

Index

A

about us 29
account history 68
  as factor in quality score 68
account history (CTR) 39
account level CTR 72
account penalties 164
account quality score 61
account-wide quality score distributions
      132–134
actual CPC 110
ad copy
  display of state or city 210
  including keywords 151
  variations 70
  writing 140, 202
  writing effective 150–152
ad copy
  CPC determination 24
  position in which it appears 23
  will it be shown 23
  writing compelling 27
  writing relevant copy 25
ad group quality score
  myth of 74
ad groups
  avoiding large 25
  narrowly focused 26
  splitting 26
  single keyword 26
  creating small 201
  how small 149
  organizing 140, 146–148
adjectives 149
ad-matching algorithm 105
ad position
  impact of quality score 103, 108–136
ad rank 108, 110, 207
  formula 108
  impact of first page bid estimate 117
  impact of landing pages 96
  impact on bid requirement 106

ad rank 57
  formula 40
adverbs 149
advertisers
  benefit from quality score 21
  driving toward best practices 20
  benefits of quality score 46
  information needed to make business deci-
        sions 41
  banned for life 93
AdWords
  quotes from help 35
  blog 35
  contacting Google 179
  extensions 128
  forums 35, 41
  help system 35, 41
  Placement/Keyword Performance Report
        123
  starting new account 183
AdWords account
  building from scratch 189
  duplicate 187
  multiple 187
AdWords API 123
AdWords Editor 123
AdWords Help Forums 181, 188
AdWords interface 122
affiliate marketing 30, 177, 181
ambiguous intent 143
AOL 78
API 123
average CPC 51
average position 202

B

B2B 168
banned advertisers 93
beer ads 20
benefit of the doubt 46
best practices 20
bid requirement 105, 106
bids
    amount you pay relative to 40
    impact of first page bid estimate 23
    impact on ad position 108
    impact on position 50
    impacting position 113
    role in calculating CPC 113
Bid Simulator 50
bots 182
bounce rates
    impact on quality score 26
Bozo
    accidental 46
    intentional 47
    tax 48
Bozo Filter 46–63
brand keywords 189
broad match 201, 209
Bruce Springsteen 87
bucket analysis 159
budget 105
business model 30, 47
    as quality score factor 22
    when Google hates it 176
    penalty 176–178, 196
business segment 30, 47
buying cycle 168
buying old AdWords accounts 73

C

campaign-level quality score
    myth of 74
Car and Driver Magazine 211
category keywords 25
clear intent 143
ClickEquations 134
ClickEquations Analyst 123, 134
click-through rate 26
    as factor in quality score 69–136
    as proxy for business success 170
    as quality score factor 22
    factors in quality score 68
    impact of ad copy 202
    impact on quality score 68
    impact on qualty score 24
    Improving 26–63
    what are high rates 27
clues
    in quality score calculation 23
competition
    impact on quality score 164, 166
competitive metrics 107
component quality scores 56
confusion 41
consumer protection service
    quality score as 47
Content Network 62
contextual alignment 24
cost per click 104
    calculation 110
    formula 114
    impact of landing pages 97
    impact of quality score 103, 110–136
    unknown cost 51
CPC. *See* cost per click
CTR
    as reported in AdWords 69
    correlation with quality score 80
    to achieve specific quality score 81
    normalized for position 77
    the secret behind relevance 83

D

deceptive offers 28
diet 177
Dimensions tab 107
Display Network 62, 78
display URL 68, 203
    as factor in quality score 68
    historical CTR 39, 79
    impact on new account 189
    impact on quality score 74
    reporting 75
DKI. *See* dynamic keyword insertion
duplicate accounts 187
dynamic keyword insertion 128, 152

E

ebooks 30
Economics of Quality Score 114
Edit Columns menu 107
Efficient Frontier 80, 131
eligibility 104, 105–136, 207
    impact of quality score 103
    tracking missed 107
Elvis Costello 209
estimated bid to show on the first page 116
exact match 59, 144, 205, 209
    use to improve CTR 27
Excel 123
exception list 170
extensions 128

F

factors that influence quality score 68–136
first page bid estimate 23, 61, 104, 116–118
    defined 116
    impact of geography 118
    impact of landing pages 97
    impact of search query 118
first page bids
    impact of quality score 103
FPBE. *See* first page bid estimate
funnel of search intent 25

G

generic keywords 25
geographic factors 68, 76–136
    impact on visible quality score 58
    influence on first page bid estimate 118
    performance 70
geographic performance 79, 209
geographic region 68
    performance as factor in quality score 39
geographic targeting 203
geographiic history 23
get-rich-quick 30, 92
Google
    as a verb 53
    assistance with this book 42
    benefit from quality score 21
    contacting 179, 182
    makes mistakes 196
    motives 20
    chief economist 99
    Software Principles 92
    Webmaster Guidelines 92
Google AdWords Help Forum 185
Google.com 62, 78
Google Network 37, 78
Google Toolbar 62

H

hair loss 177
Hal Varian 99, 102
high quality score
    benefits 127
historical account CTR 3historical CTR
    from other advertisers 23
    of account 9, 68, 70, 72–136, 79, 146, 184
    of the display URL 70
    of the keyword 70
historical CTR of the display URL 68
    as factor in quality score 68
home mortgage 53
horizontal relevance 87
horrible 175
human reviewer 182
human subjectivity 19

I

impression share 107, 207
impression share exact match 107
industry penalty 196
integer 60
intent 140, 143
irrelevant content 92

K

keyword
  associating with intent 143
  by parts of speech 149
  choosing 140, 142–143
  competition with other advertisers 23
  expansion 204, 204–207
  generic 25
  grouping 161
  historical CTR 79
  impact on new account 189
  impact on quality score 164
  in ad copy 151
  is it worth fixing? 200
  long tail 210
  minimum bid 106
  mission critical 173
  negative 204
  new 211
  options for managing quality score 171
  organizing into ad groups 146–148
  pausing or deleting 27, 213
  profitability 168
  quality score perspectives 167
  relevance 39
  relevance to ad group 68
  relevance to search query 68
  resolving overexpansion 165
  split into multiple versions 209
  under-performing 146
  unprofitable 173
  when to keep with low quality score 169
  when too targeted 210
keyword + ad copy combinations 71
keyword + ad copy CTR 70
  creating report 71
Keyword Analysis page 116
keyword diagnosis 95, 122
keyword expansion 190

Keywords Tab in AdWords 122
keyword status dialog box 179

L

landing page
  creating 141
  delivering great experience 153–154
  factors 68
  frequency of review 97
  generic 26
  impact of keywords 84
  impact on ad rank 96
  load time status 95
  penalties 28–29, 153
  penalty 164, 196, 199
  problems 176
  quality 39, 68
Landing Page and Site Quality Guidelines
    91
landing page quality 61, 90–92, 146
  impact on first page bid estimate 117
  reporting 94
  update frequency 135
lifetime advertiser ban 29
lifetime batting average 72
lifetime CTR 73. *See* historical click-
    through rate
linguistic analysis 83
logarithmic scale 115
long tail keywords 145
long-tail keywords 210
Lost IS (budget) 107
Lost IS (rank) 107
low quality score
  when to not pause or delete 169
low quality scores explained 164
low search volume 212

M

male enhancement 177
management principles 172–173
market segment
  as quality score factor 22
match type 59
maximum CPC 51
MCC 187
medical products 30
minimum bid. *See* bid requirement
minimum bid estimate. *See* first page bid
      estimate
misleading offers 28
modified broad match 144
modified text ads
  impact on quality score 72
money
  cost due to quality score 24
  saved by quality score 24
mortgage refinancing 20
moving quality scores 192
mssion-critical keywords 173
multiple accounts 187
MyClientCenter 187
mystery 41

N

negative keywords 204, 205
  to improve click-through rate 27
new keywords
  process of calculating qualty score 23
new text ads
  impact on quality score 72
no clear intent 143
non-brand keywords 126
No Problems
  laind page status 95
  landing page quality score 123
  relevance rating 85
normalized for position 77
nouns 149

O

opaque
  quality score is really 49
Oprah 126
optimize
  vs optimal 52
original content 29
other factors 39, 68
  in quality score calculation 22

P

page load time 29, 92, 95, 200
PageRank 57
parts of speech 149
penalties 100
  avoiding 28–63
  landing page 146
  site quality 28
Philadelphia 88
phrase match 144, 201, 205
Pizza 20
Placement/Keyword Performance Report
      123
policy violations 94
Poor
  landing page quality 94
  landing page quality score 97, 98, 123
  landing page rating 200
  landing page ratings 181
  landing pages 179
  relevance 199
  Relevance 123
  relevance rating 85
Poor landing page rating 30
poor user experience 29
pop-ups 29
position 104
  impact on click-through rate 202
prediction
  quality score as 21
privacy policy 29, 92
product ads 128
profit 169
profitability 168
punishing bad behavior 20

Q

quality score
    account 61
    application 103
    a real number 60
    asking Google for forgiveness 178
    benefit to good advertisers 46
    bucket analysis 159–162
    component 56
    CPC 207
    CTR correlation 80
    defined 19
    defined by Google 36
    distribution 131
    distribution graph 132
    factors 39, 68
    for ad rank 56, 207
    for CPC 56
    formula 39
    goals 162
    how factors are weighted 102
    how it helps advertisers 38
    how it helps Google 38
    how it helps searchers 38
    how it impacts your account 40
    how it's calculated 21, 67
    impact of landing pages 90
    impact on bid requirement 106
    impact on CPC 114–115
    impact on position 50
    improving 24
    interaction with bid 51
    landing page 61
    management 158
    moving between accounts 192
    numeric range 60
    penalties 28–63
    refining the formula 42
    relative weight of factors 99
    reporting window 122
    text ad 62
    the evolving nature of 22
    update frequency 135
    versions 39
    visible 56
    what are good 31
    what the number mean 124–129
    when it won't improve 196

    where it is used 23
    why Google has it 37
    why they're low 164
quality score for ad rank 56
quality score for CPC 56
quality score formula
    rigidity 23
quality score penalties 100
Qual. Score column 122
quarantined 191
query mining 204–207
questions
    not answering them 52

R

rank 104
ranking
    impact of quality score 103
ranking ads
    impact of quality score 108
real number 60, 115
redirects 29
rehab 185
relevance 39, 68, 82–136, 199
    as factor in quality score 68
    as quality score factor 22
    defined 82
    dictionary definition 83
    of the keyword 68
    of the matched ad 68
    other factors 68
    ratings 85
    what it means 22
restarting a new account 186
revenue attribution 168
rewarding good behavior 20
rotate
    text ad option 70

S

satisfaction
  of advertisers 21
  of Google 21
  of searchers 21
searchers
  benefit from quality score 21
  disrespecting 28
Search Network 36, 62
search query 27, 105
  aligning with ad copy 24
  dynamic keyword insertion 152
  impact on quality score 201
  impact on visible quality score 58
  influence on first page bid estimate 118
  matching to keywords 146
  non-identical to keyword 59
  relevance 39
  reports 205
  reviewing 27
  role of relevance 84
search results
  without paid ads 88
secret sauce
  quality score as 49
semantic analysis 83
Sex 20
Siddharth Shah 80, 131
sitelinks 128
site quality 91
  reporting 94
site quality policy violations 29
site suspended 95
small ad groups 149
Software Principles 92
Status Window in AdWords 122
structural problems 164
  resolving 165

T

target URL
  historical CTR 146
technical problems 164
tension 41
text ad. *See* Ad copy
text ad quality score 62
text ads
  alone on a page 116
  average CTR 71
  display of state or city 210
  impact of changes on quality score 72
  impact of performance differences 70
  keywords with no ads 88
thought bubble 85, 122
three strikes and you're out 47
tightly focused ad groups 140
top position 109, 127
traditional marketing channels 142
transparency 52
  desired 49
tricking people 20

U

uncertainty 41
unprofitable keywords 173
user experience 94

V

verbs 149
versions of quality score 39
vertical relevance 86
Viagra 177
visible CTR 79
visible quality score 56, 124
  details 57–63
  impact of low CTR ad copy 71
  update frequency 58, 197
visible URL. *See* display URL
  generic 26
  signaling relevance 26

W

Webmaster Guidelines 92
weighted average of the CTR 71
weighting of quality score factors 22
whole number 60
wisdom of the crowd 69

Y

YouTube video 102

25407423R00124

Made in the USA
Columbia, SC
30 August 2018